A Time to Walk

Jewel Sweeney

Sweeney Publishing ©2017

ISBN 9781546881766

Dedication

To my family and friends that encouraged me to write this and speak through my fears, thank you for sticking by me. A special thanks to my husband for editing and putting up with me. To the church families that I've been a part of, ministers, small groups, brothers and sisters in Christ who have helped open my eyes to see truth, thank you for doing your job for the growth of the Kingdom.

To God be the Glory!

Special thanks to my pastor for using phrases that were perfect for chapter titles.

Table of Contents

Welcome

Have you ever had that itch you can't scratch? Well, this is mine. Over the past decade I have been journaling and writing about topics within the church. Many of my pieces are inspired from truths that God teaches me one on one. Some are sparked from conversations, things I've read, or things I've seen in people in my life. When I began, I felt the call to create a book from what God was teaching me, but I felt an overwhelming feeling of doubt. Who am I to speak as though I am speaking for God? What right do I have? Who would listen to me anyway?

Well, time went on and I kept writing here and there. Doubt took hold and fear governed my life. Then, two years ago, I began to write other works. I wrote a novel and began working on children's picture books. As I dove into writing, I began to get back into writing on the spiritual issues at hand again. It was almost as if I needed a kickstart. I needed to be reminded to write.

As doors began to open, and pieces fell into place, I began to see that I was to speak. God has given me his words to remind myself and others about a variety of things, and it is my job to share them, not horde them all for myself and my family. I began a blog as a way to speak some truth into the world around me, but I knew from the start, it wasn't what God wanted from me.

So here we have it. This is a compilation of pieces written between the years 2004 and 2017. They have been edited, re-written, re-tooled to fit in what we (my husband and I) feel to be most impactful, and helpful. This was written to be used as a reminder/devotional. Though you, as a reader, could do one a day, I feel it might be better to work through one a week. Read it. Think on it. Pray on it. Use each piece as a guide to find more. Take out your Bible and find passages that come alongside of the piece. I'm not one to baby people. I'm not forcing anyone to read this. So I refuse to spoon feed. Yes, there are scriptural references in many pieces, but read them for yourself. Read the scriptures in different translations of the Bible. I used a NASB for my references to keep things consistent, though in my house you will also find me using NIV and ESV.

I entitled the book "A Time to Walk" because throughout my life I have found solace in walking. The time with nature and what God has given us clears my head, reveals truth, and brings peace. We talk about our relationship with God as our walk with Him. I find it appropriate on so many levels. We can only run once we have been conditioned, and only for a time. We cannot crawl forever. But we can walk. We do it daily. Little bits at a time, or long distances. Walking is continuous, and along a chosen path. We can all walk further on the path each day.

I pray that this work brings truth to hearts that are open and willing. I hope that this brings challenges that invoke seeking the Lord above. It is my desire that those who choose to read this will fall in love with the God of all and run the race set before them with fire and passion.

Many Blessings,
Jewel Sweeney

Dreamin' Big

My mother bought me a fitness journal. I've never had one before, but I figured I would give it a try. It's pretty cool. It gives you a place for goals and motivation. It's set up in a before and after style, to check in. I usually do the after the next morning because by the time the day is over I do not feel like journaling. On one page it gives you a "motivational" saying. From there you can journal. One morning the saying was, "Goals are dreams with deadlines." Interesting. But for some reason, I focused on the dream part.

Dreams, though they are, can be achieved. Give them time. Walk within them. God will give us the desires of our hearts, if we will just walk with Him. See Him for who He is. He loves us. Let that sink in. The God of all loves us. He sees us as his children and just wants us. He wants us. He wants to walk with us. He wants to sit with us and speak with us. So dream. Dream big. Let your heart go wild. He knows what you want. Just speak it. Let him in on it. Let Him work on you to get you to where you need to be to reach this dream and walk in it. But you must let Him walk with you in it.

That was what I journaled one sleepy morning. Then a funny thing happened. The same day, just an hour or so later, I received an email. You can probably guess where this was going. It involved an opportunity of growth with my children's book. So what did I do? I questioned it. I wondered which way to go. I emailed my husband, texted my mom, texted the neighbor, and talked to whomever I could find asking for prayer and advice. *What do I do*?! Really? Later that evening I showed my husband the journal entry above. He said, "Yup."

There's a big point within that journal entry. Proverbs says that God will give us the desire of our hearts. And he does. You see, when we walk with God and let Him into every part of our lives we create a oneness with Him. That's the best part of a marriage. When you and your spouse are on the same page about decisions, it makes life easier. That's how it is with God. When we have a deep relationship with him, we have the same mindset. Our desires are His desires. The things we want to do with our lives, the way we choose to interact with others, how we spend our time, all seem to blend with how God wants us to do those things. It's easy for God to give us the desires of our hearts when our desires are His desires.

This book, and every other book I write and have written, is a dream come true. There are pieces I wish to write that didn't make it to the book. There are pieces that I didn't want to write, but knew the Holy Spirit was leading me to write. I've wanted to write for as long as I could remember. Opportunities have come and gone. It wasn't until I reached the point of bringing God into my writing that something great happened. Walking with God brought more desire to write. My writing became inspired. My desire became more focused. No longer was I someone who wrote on the side, it became a priority.

It becomes that way for whatever it is that you dream and desire. When you dream of being a teacher, you can teach. That's easy enough. Get a degree, get the certification, go to a career fair. There's a great need for teachers, always. But if you don't walk with God on your path to becoming a teacher, it makes it more difficult. You can do well. You can pass classes, and move on to be a fine teacher. After a few years (maybe less) you lose your fire. You're frustrated by paperwork, kids, parents, and everything else. That desire to do good in the world has washed away and you feel hopeless. However, if God is with you and walking along side of you it makes more sense. Sure, it's still difficult. Yes, people and tasks make you want to leave your job, but you are willing to suffer through it for those good moments. You deal with the pressures, the low pay, and the conferences for the chance to change the lives of the kids that walk into your classroom.

Goals may be dreams with deadlines, but dreams are the desires of our heart. We try to hide these things from God. We put them aside like they are silly and we are just children playing pretend. That isn't what He wants. Our God, the one who loves us deeply, wants to live in our dreams with us. He wants us to pursue those "silly things" we wanted to be when we were kids, before the world beat us down and told us to run from it. If there is something that you want, spend time with God. If it is worth pursuit, God will open doors, focus you, bring changes, show the path bit by bit. It won't be easy. You will be tested. But when you continue to dream, walk with God, and work, you can reach your dreams and allow those dreams to grow.

Dreams

This is the first time I have put pen to paper when it comes to this experience. Perhaps I feared judgment. Perhaps I feared truth. Perhaps I didn't deem it important, which I have now.

Let me set the scene. I am 18, a freshman at Charleston Southern University. One roommate was a volleyball player so she had been on campus before us and settled in. She was gone for the night, most likely for a match. The other roommate grew up just miles from the campus. She dropped some things and left to stay at her mother's house. It was a typical night for me. One roommate out for sports, friends, or boyfriend. The other home for whatever reason. Night after night I would have the room to myself, especially on weekends.

So here I am, alone in my room, ready for bed. I close the blinds because outside our room is a bright street light. I go to bed and fall asleep without a problem. Then I have this dream:

I'm in my church back home, except it's built up more with a large balcony all around. There was some sort of concert going on. We were grouped as a youth group, at least in my mind, but I didn't recognize any of the people in my group. As the concert went on, I caught the eye of a young man. He was gorgeous. Completely out of my league. I couldn't believe he was even looking at me. He leaned over and whispered to his friend. We were so far apart I couldn't read his lips, but somehow I knew he was talking about me.

We all cleared out of the church/auditorium. Our group piled onto a school bus. Sure enough his security guard best friend had saved a seat for me. After I sat, the gorgeous young man sat next to me. I immediately felt both trapped by him, but amazed that he chose me. We sat and talked. I was sucked in to every word he said. There was a nagging feeling that something wasn't right, but I kept ignoring it. (You know, like when you date someone that isn't right for you, but you think it's better to be with someone for now than to be alone.)

So the bus stops at my grandparents' house. (Background, they were still alive at this time of my life. I have countless memories of family gatherings. I lived there with my family for a few months while our house was being built, and would get dropped off on a bus just like that. That home and yard, have always meant so much to me.) I get off the bus, along with Mr. Handsome and his lackey. My grandparents' dirt driveway was empty as it curved around the small flower garden. We walked past the side of the house. There was a small tree between their house and the neighbor's property. This tree was always the indicator of a touchdown in family football games as passing it, you passed into the endzone. The back yard was quite large. To the end of the clearing, there was a small hill we would go sledding on in the winter. To the left, at the neighbor's property, there was a fence where they had a few animals. In my dream, there were rams- I didn't understand it in my dream either.

The gorgeous unnamed guy was talking to me. We went to the fence. A ram turned and looked to us. You could see the agitation in its eyes. The guy and his friend mocked the ram, knowing he was held within the fence. The ram began to run towards us. The guys laughed and walked away down the small hill, through sparse trees and back to the freshly cut grass of my grandparents' yard.

We talked as we walked and gorgeous guy told me he wanted me to be with him. I was shocked. He put his arm around me. This is where I began to realize what was happening. This guy had charmed me. He knew I was drawn to him. When he had me alone he gave me the ultimatum. He wanted me to give up everything I loved. As I debated the decision, the ram made its way out. He charged down the hill. The friend was overtaken by the ram and laid helplessly on the ground. The ram came after hot guy, smooth talker. They fought and wrestled. Back and forth they went. I ran to the small tree. This time I didn't run past to the endzone, but climbed within its branches. I watched the battle in fear. Deep within me I knew the truth. The ram knew that I couldn't give up everything. The ram knew that the beautiful light the gorgeous guy offered was going to keep me from the world I knew – a life worth living, a life of purpose. Was I willing to give up Christ for this guy?

My gorgeous dream guy had his hands on the ram's horns. They were locked in a battle. He gritted his teeth, dug his toes into the yard (how dare he mess up my grandfather's mowing), and turned his head to me. "You can't have both! You cannot be with him and me. You must choose!"

I woke up with an intense fear. The room was completely dark, which was unusual. Typically the light peeked through the blinds, but this time there was nothing. It was a heavy blackness. At that time I realized I had people in my life that were driving me away from the Lord. It was "only" a small distraction, but immediately I heard the truth. "No one can serve two masters." (Matt 6:24) And again I pictured a scene of this scripture, "Away from me, Satan! For it is written, 'Worship the Lord your God and serve him only.'" (Matt. 4:10) Gulp. I spoke those words over and over, "Away from me Satan! I am a child on the King. Jesus is with me!" The darkness cleared and light came back from under the door, then around the blinds.

That dream stuck with me for a long time. It was so clear. Just as the Bible says, Satan comes as the angel of light. He draws us in many ways, but at the end he will snarl at you to make a decision. Hopefully, we each choose correctly.

Y'all Ain't Ghetto Like Me

Can I ask you a question? This is an honest question. When I ask you this question, I want you to stop and truly answer before you continue on reading. Ready? Who are you? Now think hard. Search deep. Answer with all sincerety. Who are you?

Did you answer? Of course, you did. I have been in quite a few interviews for career moves. Of course, the first question inevitably is, "So tell me, who is Jewel?" Yikes. I usually try the "Oh, who knows!" with a nervous laugh. They usually smile and say nothing, hinting that that might not be the best joke at the time. Naturally, I'm just buying time to figure out exactly what to say.

Now, walk down the street and ask somebody that same question, and I'm sure the majority of people will say the same type of thing. Honestly, I'm sure the majority of you answered the same way. The majority of Americans answer the question like this: Me? I am a... Fill in the blank – doctor, lawyer, teacher, mother, student, athlete, therapist... You get the idea.

So, did you answer my question that way? Did you say that you were a teacher? Did you say you were a loving spouse? Maybe you're a proud parent. What was the question? "Who." Who are you? Not "what do you do?" It wasn't about who you associate yourself with, but who you are.

This is a difficult question. How are you supposed to answer it without saying what you do or who you are with? I often struggle with this and Christian mothers. Ask me about who they (we) are and I will say, "They're crazy! They are godly women who love their families and have spent their lives devoted to both God and family." I see this as a good and bad thing together. The good thing about Christian mothers is that they are God fearing. Their faith is seen in their life. The second part is what scares me. Their life becomes devoted to their family-husband and children. Now I know what you're thinking, I'm nuts. Why is loving your family and taking care of them such a bad thing? All mothers should be that way. Absolutely. All mothers should love and care for their families. But is that as far as it goes? What would they be if they no longer were wives or mothers? How then would they identify themselves?

Let me give a personal example: People often with pointless differences. You see, I am athletic. I love fitness and sports. I was always a "tom-boy," though I hate the term. My mother is the opposite. She is crafty and artistic. Though I shared no interest in participating with her in weaving or crocheting, I do respect her ability to perform these works of arts. That being said, my mother may have felt as though I did not care for her because I did not care for crafts. (I do indeed care for crafts and have myself picked up many since this time of writing.) My mother feigned interest and pretended to care about what I cared about, even though it wasn't her. Part of her changed and adapted to the people around her so that they might appreciate her more.

Now let's go back to you. Do you do this? We always think of teenagers and peer pressure, but it doesn't go away with age. We all want to be accepted every last one of us. So each day we do what we can to feel a little bit of love from someone, anyone. We all tell ourselves we don't. We don't care what others think or say about us, but we do. Or at least until we are comfortable in whom we are. Ay, there's the rub! Or something like that. When are we comfortable with ourselves? When do we accept our personal identity? Never! Well, that is, until you accept your identity in Christ. I know, it sounds so cliché, and I'm completely sorry for that, but it is the truth. We will do all that we can to win approval of others, but when we accept the approval and grace of God we are freed from the approval of man.

So I ask you again, who are you? Are you a child of God? My mother is a proud wife and mother, and she acts in such a manner. She reflects it. However, she is first and foremost a child of God. And she reflects that and acts like it. Are you reflecting God? We are told day after day that we are to be ourselves. Express who we are. So let's do that. If you are a singer, sing. If an artist, create. If an athlete, compete. But do so without them taking over your identity. When someone asks you who you are, do you respond with what you do, or what you've accomplished? Tell them who you are. Royalty by God's hand. Take pride in that for once. Not in your salary, car, or even as wonderful as they are, your family.

The Crew

Out of the many reasons to love Jesus, there is one example that fits right into my wheelhouse. The way Jesus kept his companions is exactly what I want in life. He walks through crowds of people trying to see him, touch him, get a nugget of truth and life from him. He teaches and works with his disciples. He chooses his favorites. Yup. That's me.

When we look at the ministry that Jesus had in just three years, he created a world where people wanted him. They knew him all throughout the area. He traveled by foot to a variety of places, villages, and even the wilderness. As he traveled to these villages, people flocked to him. His hometown tried to kill him, yes, but there was still a crowd. Many of the Jewish people wanted to see their future King. They didn't understand how he would have to lay down his life. They didn't know that he wouldn't start the revolution against the Roman government. It didn't matter where he went, people wanted to see him. Doesn't that sound like the rock star status that we all secretly want? We all want to be noticed. We would love for crowds to flock to us, knowing exactly who we are and the things we could do.

Even though the crowds were around him, he chose 12 to be His disciples. How many of us have 12 friends? Probably most of us. These weren't His only friends. Lazurus, Mary, and Martha were also his friends. However, not one of them was considered one of his direct disciples. He knew he had to pour into those 12. If the group were to get too large, he wouldn't be able to give them the attention they needed. But also, those were the 12 he needed to have. Just because someone is our friend, it doesn't mean they are the people we are supposed to take into our inner circle. We should always be showing God's love to those we come across, however, God gives us a select few that become our 12; our group that we pour into and bring truth to. Those we need to share some of our deeper and more intimate teachings with.

After we have our group of people that we know we pour into, there comes the innermost circle. Jesus took John, James, and Peter with him further into the garden to pray. John was called "the beloved." Jesus had crowds. He had friends. He had disciples. Then he had his best friends. These are the guys he wanted by his side if he was to go into battle. These were the three that knew his deep dark secrets. We have these friends. For many adults our spouse is one of them. We may have that best friend that knows everything before we say it. Jesus chose three as His go to guys. I like that number. A group of four means partners. There's always someone to talk to.

Ecclesiates 4 says that two are better than one, and that a cord of three cannot be broken. So what can a cord of four do? Surely that is even stronger. But after that, we lose intimacy. Add one more person and we have an odd man out. Put in two more, now there's a crowd. Jesus chose his three as a perfect example. So what if we go the other direction? Let's say he only chose the sons of Zebedee, John and James. Now we're back to odd man out. Now they're playing favorites. I've had that before. It's difficult on all sides. Maybe he only chose Peter as his BFF. Now the other ten (leaving out Judas) would be wondering what makes Peter so special?

In our world things may be a little different. Having just one person to confide in can be difficult if they aren't available. Maybe sometimes they give poor advice, or don't have the knowledge or experience needed to help. They, or you, might get tired of each other teaching the lessons of Christ. We were meant to have more. More support, more minds, more to share our wisdom with. Having that group of three that know what you need are truly important.

In the end, Jesus needed one person. He needed his heavenly father. He longed to be with him. He longed to be back in the heavenly realm with his father, overseeing it all. But when we look in John 17, we see Jesus prayed to his father for those disciples. He worried over them. He wanted to set them up to continue the good works they had been doing, which ends up being more than they expected to do. And though he wanted them to be safe and secure, his heart was already with his father. We need that relationship. We need that longing. That desire to be one with the Father. Once we have that fulfillment with God, we can move within the crowds, pour into our twelve, and live deeply with our three.

Reading the Bible

Why do you read the Bible? Why do any of us read the Bible? Why should we read the Bible? What is the point of it all? I have been known to been struggling with the purpose behind reading it all. I have grown up in the church and have been taught everything there is to know about how and why to study the Bible. But sometimes I feel that it's all wrong. It's pointless.

Let's answer the first questions I asked. We read the Bible to learn. I have been taught on a consistent basis to read the Bible to find answers. We use it to answer the questions of this world. What should I do when someone hits me? Old Testament: eye for an eye. New Testament: turn the other cheek. So which is it? We are the New Testament church, right? So turn the other cheek. How I should act, what I should wear, who I should marry, how I should raise my children, it's all in there. Every scenario. But the trouble with that theory is that it's incomplete. Paul wrote most of the books in the New Testament. But he wrote letters to church groups in Europe and Asia 2000 years ago. How is it that the answer written in the book of Romans is the exact answer for me?

So why do we read the Bible? Well, we are to hide his Word in our hearts. The Bible is His Word. Therefore, we read the Bible to learn it and keep it in our hearts so that we won't sin against God. But I challenge this. The Bible is indeed God breathed and his Word, but is it His *only* Word? I think not. There are many times that God speaks outside of the Bible. Someone filled with the Holy Spirit often speaks truth into peoples' lives. Sometimes it is from the scriptures or similar ideas, and sometimes it isn't. Have you ever written or received a note of encouragement from a fellow Christian? Is that not a word from God? Did you hide that encouragement in your heart? Or did you brush it aside and go back to the easy way?

God speaks to us all the time. He speaks in many different ways. And He speaks to each of us in our own way. When this concept hit me, I cannot express the freedom I felt. I do not enjoy reading. I sometimes have a hard time sitting down alone with a Bible and reading. I've done so many different ways of studying. Read one passage, meditate on it for thirty minutes and then find out what it says to you. What? It didn't say anything. It was genealogy. So... ok... Jesus came from the line of David. That means: he was man. So I should strive to be perfect because Jesus was a man? Now I need to focus on this all day. How is that supposed to work? Ok, there is the method of reading a chapter and picking what works for you. Or the best one- read the verses that will help you directly. Something bothering you? "I'm pressed, but not crushed; persecuted, not abandoned." Now I feel better. Don't know what will help? Use the keyword search in the back of your Bible. That will help. Do a different study. Take notes as you read. Star the verses that speak to you. Highlight in your Bible.

Do, do, do and you will get, get, get. Because we are selfish. Yes, I said it. We are selfish. Examine yourself right now. Why do you read the Bible? Is it because you were looking to find an answer? It is the number one reason we are taught to read the Bible. Pastors sing it from the pulpits "Read and find out what it is saying to you." You know what often it says to me? This is what happened thousands of years ago to this group of people and this is how it was handled.

So I come to today. What happens to me when I go out in nature with God? When I sit in quiet or speak with Him? He speaks to me. His Word comes to me outside of the Bible. I always knew it, but felt like a failure for not being able to sit and read the Bible for hours at a time. But it's okay. He reaches me in a different way. I'm not saying those who study the Word are wrong. If He speaks to you that way, great. If not, it's alright. How does he speak to you? Some people encounter God through music. Others through other people. And ultimately, I believe that God speaks to each one of us in different ways.

Why then do we read the Bible? Why should we? Let's look at first century Christians; those that knew Christ himself. What Bible did they read? They read the Old Testament books. But Christ came to be the New Covenant. Why bother reading the Old Testament? I truly believe in my heart of hearts that they read scriptures to learn about God. They read His promises. They read about His love. They read about His wrath. They studied God. And when you study *who* God is, you learn His ways. You learn His mindset. You learn Him. And, when you learn God, you have no choice but to love God. And when you love God, truly know and love God, you do what is right. Not because Paul wrote it, but because you know and feel it is what God wants of you. You serve out of a loving heart. You love others because you know the love of God.

So we read the Bible. We read the promises of God. We need to see how unchanging, forgiving, and powerful our God is. But when we find God, we know that He will speak to us. He may speak through another medium, but He wants to speak to us directly. If you're looking for an answer, ask Him the question. He may show you the answer in our man bound book of words to past Christians, but He may not. Let Him give you an answer directly. And read His Word to know Him more.

Internal Organs

We are all a part of the spiritual body of Christ. Paul in 1 Corinthians 12 talks about the various parts of a body. Each part has something to do. And without just one small part, the body is not whole. I've always looked at this passage and thought, "What part am I?"

Paul uses this analogy of a functioning body to describe how spiritual gifts are distributed amongst the church. Not one member will have all the gifts, and thus, we need all the church body to work together to function properly. He even goes and lists out the members of God's body: apostles, prophets, teachers, miracle workers, healers, helpers, administrators, speakers of various kinds of tongues. Ok. So where am I? Apostle-foot. Prophet-mouth. Teacher-brain. So on and so forth. I see how people can become physical body parts.

Over the years I've taken the tests to determine my spiritual gifts. My top gifts are always wisdom, discernment, and leadership. The first time I saw that I wanted to puff out my chest and flare some peacock feathers. (I was 19 and thought to be wise, who wouldn't be excited?) Through time I've been able to see how these gifts have played out in my life. However, I find it difficult to use with the rest of the church body. I often feel like I know the truth about people long before they have a clue. Should I then walk up to them, or their spouse, and say, "Hey, I've noticed there's a problem with you. Let me help!"? How could I? Instead, I noticed where I can help, in prayer. My spirit can say what needs to be said. Sometimes I've prayed with people and specifically asked for something. They were in shock. "How did you know?" is the typical reaction. "God told me," is the easiest response.

So what am I? The brain filled with wisdom? I don't think so. You see, I've been in the church my entire life. And maybe it's just my liberal use of my gift of discernment, but I think I have a different way to look at our spiritual Church body than the traditional teachings. Let's start with the big three: God the Father, Jesus, and the Holy Spirit. Paul says again that the church is the body and he says that "Christ is the head of the church, the body..." (Col 1:18). Done, no need to interpret that. I believe God is the heart. Some might argue that God should be the head and Christ the heart, but I don't think it holds up as well. I want God's heart. Without it we would have his wrath.

I don't want, nor do I need, His wealth of knowledge. It's too much for me, or any human. However, I would like Jesus' knowledge. He was in our flesh and never sinned. What's the trick? How did He handle the emotions? Ok, we know the answers, but don't you want to sit down for a cup of coffee with Him and ask how to be angry without sinning?

I digress. God is also the heart because we can live with artificial hearts. Think about it. Today people have parts of pig hearts and pacemakers. In the church body this would translate as not a God heart, but a god heart. The Holy Spirit is the veins and arteries. Without the circulatory system what is in the heart doesn't make it to the rest of the body. Also, the trash in the cells doesn't get flushed out. I'm sure some of you just said, "What? Circulatory system? Why not lungs? Breath of Life, duh!" I hear you. I do. But really, we can get air in multiple sources, but that circulatory system is necessary to move that oxygen to the body.

The lungs and airways are for the pastors and teachers. They provide the body with the Word and Life. If your church is struggling to breathe, you could find oxygen from a new pastor, online podcasts, televised services, books and so much more. It would be like having an oxygen tank instead of a greater lung capacity, but still does the job.

I look around my church to see what other body parts are moving. I see the feet- these are the people who go to the same village in Ethiopia every year bringing the gospel. I see one woman and think, "She's a knee." A knee? Yeah, I said it. She is in the prayer room outside the chapel each Sunday praying for, with, and over people. Without her lowering herself in prayer there would be more people struggling to stand. I wish I could be a knee, but it's not me. We have hands that are working, healing. They pull and push. The hands get blisters that turn to calluses and the skin is stronger for the toil. Those are the most obvious members of the body to see and understand.

So where does that put the rest of us? Where does that put me? Recently I figured out where I am in the Body of Believers. I'm intestines. Did I get your attention? Ok, so some of us are intestines. I love it, now that I recognize it. I'm steady. I'm constant. There are times when my job is to help food be digested and getting nutrients absorbed. Other times I have to help push the crap out. But I'm there. Throughout my many years of church attendance- you know, from birth on- I have been in choirs, sang in cantatas. I have been a youth leader and a youth pastor. I have worked with children's churches and VBS's. I've performed on drama teams and led Bible studies. I've been disciple and have discipled. I've helped people get their nutrients of Spirit soaked Bread of Life, and I've pushed away false teachings. The food may come in a variety of formats- chips and soda: youth group, graham crackers and apple juice: children's church, donuts and coffee: Bible study- but it all gets digested as necessary. And when the Church body has trouble in the gut the whole body knows it. There may be some gas or even reflux. Sometimes the Word flows through too quickly and sometimes we can't get past a part. The body can feel the uneasiness within.

So maybe you aren't in the guts. You may be the arm that keeps the hand moving. You may be the leg that connects to the foot and allows it to walk. Without muscle strength and endurance the hands and feet are rendered useless. The hand cannot touch what the arm won't stretch out to. Moses needed help from Aaron and Hur raising his arms to defeat the Amalekites. They were his muscle.

Some of you make up the skin. Maybe you're the one keeping sickness and infection from the rest of the body. Sure you have scrapes, scratches and scars, but each one is a time that you fought for the preservation of the body and succeeded. Each scar is different. Some took longer to heal than others. But you protected us. And those scars will be shown off like trophies when the time comes.

Two thousand years ago Paul taught the church to be a body; to move and work together. I used to be jealous of the hands. I was afraid to be a foot. Now I look at myself and know where I am. I'm happy to be in the gut of the body. I'm still important, even when nobody thinks about me.

Timing

Have you ever noticed how God's timing is nowhere close to ours? At this moment I should be in bed. In addition to work tomorrow, I have a huge interview. Honestly, I didn't even want to be awake at this time, but for some reason I decided to watch TV and get on the computer. I hopped onto Facebook. One of my (now former) athletes requested friendship. I approved and viewed her profile. At that time, I noticed she had a drama video on her page from her church. I have seen the drama before and it touched me deeply. So I chose to watch it, then I added it to my own profile for other to see. To watch it, still hits deep. However the song that it is performed to has been a favorite of mine. The song is "Everything" by Lifehouse. The chorus of the song says:

"How can I stand here with you and not be moved by you? Would you tell me, 'How could it be any better than this?' Cus' you're all I want. You're all I need. You're everything. Everything."

The entire song is a cry of the heart. It's a longing to be with him. I hear it and feel nothing but romance and passion that's inside of it.

So I watched the video and put that CD in. I sat back on the couch, watched five minutes of TV and was completely restless. So I went to bed with the thought that I would fall asleep listening to the song on repeat. God had a different idea. He wanted to break me.

I listened to the song and wanted nothing more than to dance with my Savior. So I did. We danced. He spun me. He turned me. He held me close. Our hearts connected. We laughed. We were brought together. And I couldn't help it. I opened my bedroom door and ran out to the living room singing: "You're all I want. You're all I need." By the time I reached, "You're everything" I was on my knees in tears. (I guess it's a good thing I lived alone.)

I've been so foolish. Searching endlessly for happiness, for joy, for love. I argue with God daily saying I need a man to fill my heart. I don't. Money won't satisfy. Clothes won't sooth. Friends don't complete me. And a man will not fulfill my everything. Only He can. Only God. Only Jesus. Only His love and compassion. Only His grace and mercy.

The only one that has ever shown the world, shown me true and honest romance is Him! Only Him. When I stand with Him I'm moved by Him. So what have I been doing? Where have I been standing? I'm not being moved! I want to move. I want to dance.

I need romance. We all do. God, let me dance with you!

Be everything, everything!

Calling and Purpose

There are so many things I want to say when it comes to finding your calling, but I often wonder if I'm the person to say it. Is there something that gets you fired up more than anything else? Are there people around you encouraging you in an endeavor? Do you feel fulfilled when you get just an ounce of doing this one thing? Why do you think that is?

I've noticed that throughout our lives we are guided into areas of our expertise, passion, and desire. I've been a jock for as long as I can remember. Fitness comes naturally to me. I love being in a gym. I love exercising. And I became a trainer because I love helping others get fit. It is a part of me that God designed. I know I will always have my hand in the fitness world in whatever capacity. But it doesn't always challenge me. If things aren't challenging, we don't grow. This is something we know from fitness.

I'm so thankful for my pastor. It is very rare that I leave a Sunday service without feeling challenged and empowered to do what God has called me to do. However, some days as I feel ready to go and change the world for the kingdom of God, I wonder if I'm doing what it is I'm supposed to do. Through Scripture, sermons, internal and external confirmations, and people, I have been able to find some answers.

God never tells us that He will pave the way for us to do what we are called to do. Rather, I have seen that we will be tested, challenged, and worked to get on and stay on the path we are called to. It's a difficult road to travel, not the easy way out. While we go through the turbulence, we hone our skills, we defend ourselves, and we prove to ourselves – and anyone else – why we are doing what we are called to do.

How you react to the challenges will show yourself what it's like. We need to be careful when these obstacles come to us. Some of the tests are just that. It's basically a pass/fail exam. Can you do this? Do you really desire to do this? When I say it's pass/fail I mean that in the barest terms. Let's say you feel it is your calling to be a party planner. A friend of yours is pregnant and you decide to throw the party. This is your first event. At the end of the shower you look back. Did you do it? Did people show up? Was your friend thankful for the party, the gifts, the thought and effort? Great. You passed. Did you have a meltdown in the middle of planning the party? So what. If you put so much effort into create a wonderful baby shower for your friend, how much more will you put in for a customer?

Just because things get difficult or you lose your mind over it, doesn't mean you aren't supposed to be right where you are. There's a song I hear on the radio by Hawk Nelson (saw them in concert early in their career and fell in love) called "Diamonds." There's a bridge that says "Oh the Joy of the Lord, It will be my strength. When the pressure is on He's making Diamonds." Wow. I love it. I love the visualization of it all. When times are tough, he's making diamonds. Something as crude as coal becomes a diamond only when there is enough pressure and heat. Are we not just the same way? Too often I see people stifled in life because they are not allowing themselves to fall into their passion. There's too much pressure to do what we are called to do. Or is the pressure just what we need?

There are few things greater than confirmation. Some of us rely on internal confirmation. We need to feel like we are doing the right thing. Some of us rely on external confirmation. We need someone to come along and tell us we are doing the right thing. I believe that when you are walking in your calling you will receive both. You will know within your heart of hearts that you are exactly where you need to be, and those around you will know and tell you.

Another piece that will fall into place is the people in your life. Sometimes you'll experience a change that makes no sense at all. Someone will leave, or you'll meet someone new. These people will help to grow the passion within you. They may have answers to your doubts and fears. They may be the ones asking the questions. No matter the situation, when these people come into your life, even if only for a time, embrace them. Work with them to develop what needs to be developed within you in order to enhance your abilities within your calling.

Little story, I bought myself one of those journaling Bibles that girls draw pretty things in for the advertisements. Well, I use it more for notes, ideas, and emphasis. I can't really draw or write with good handwriting, let alone the pretty swirly stuff. About a month ago I was flipping through the pages and saw the places I had doodled something in colored pencil (I have to make it pretty somehow). Countless times I had the word "speak" written out. Over and over I had read and felt the call to speak out, to tell the truth, to speak to help, to say what must be said. Well, look where we are now.

Fear

If there is anyone who knows fear, it's God. Hear me out. Genesis, God creates man and knows it isn't good for him to be alone (when fear creeps in) and He makes woman. In Joshua it is written, "Be strong and courageous" four times in the first chapter. Opposite of courage, fear. Jesus in the Garden of Gethsemine asks for the cup to be taken from him because He knew what was coming. And Paul reminds Timothy his fellow worker to have courage, not a spirit of fear.

Fear is nothing new. Countless poets, writers, and songwriters tell us just how crippling fear is. For some reason I had a difficult time understanding why fear cripples people. I guess that teenage mindset of invincibility thing just decided to stick around, or show up late. I've never felt that rush of invincibility. I was far too grounded as a young adult to be outrageous. I know, I missed out on a range of stupidity. I'm saving it for my midlife crisis. It took me quite some time to understand why people would allow for fear to "cripple them." I guess my mindset is just different in the choice of words. "Allowing" fear to win. I'll get to that later.

When people asked me what I feared I never really had a solid answer. I fear losing my family, but who doesn't? You don't hole yourselves up for the rest of your lives. If I lost my home to a storm, I could rebuild. Injuries heal. If my husband left (it would stink) but life would go on. We figure out that we can and must live life despite the fears. It's fight or flight, right?

So how can fear cripple? It's the other parts of life that take over. Will I ever find love? Fear of being alone keeps us locked up. Will I get a good degree and job? Now we aren't even applying to schools. There is this overwhelming fear of failing in this world. Any topic. Any issue. We are crippled when we fear failure.

That was the understanding I came to when it came to my writing. For years I hid my passion to put pen to paper. I didn't want people to judge what I did. I knew that if I opened myself up to let people read my words there would be someone who didn't like what I said. There would be someone who thought I couldn't hack it. There would be a reason to quit and give up on my dream. However, the thought of rejection didn't cripple me at first. I could hide it long enough. But once my first writings made it to others- fear set in. Sending my work to publishers is the scariest things I've ever done. I've been rejected. It is miserable. I am left with a choice – do I keep writing and sending out, do I keep writing but don't send out, or do I stop writing all together? For about a month I stopped. All I thought about was my failures.

The problem with thinking about your failures is that it becomes an avalanche. One failure reminds you of another failure. That reminds you of another blotch on your record. Those lead you to mistakes made. Then we take things that weren't failures and we see them as such. Finally, we take one look at ourselves and say that we are the failure. Everything we do is wrong. The past thoughts and memories crush us under their weight. The next time an opportunity is set before us we don't even try. We assume we know the outcome- failure.

Once you have failed so many times you have this fear you'll do it again. Sometimes we hit the point of acceptance. "Why bother? I know I'm not going to make it happen. I'm just going to fail at this like everything else." But still, we don't want to fail. Deep within ourselves we're hoping for more. We hope to overcome the long line of failures.

So we sit back, trapped by our fear, not going anywhere, not doing anything. That just isn't the way to live. Should we fail? Well, we probably will a time or two in any situation, but we won't know the outcome until we try. We can't fear what is out in the world for us. How many things would we miss out on if we lived each decision on the side of fear? My life would be completely different. And though I have had failure after failure, at least by worldly standards, I would not have the knowledge, experience, strength and joy that I have now in my success.

Fear is inevitable. However, God has created ways for us to move outside of that fear and conquer. Hebrews 2:14-15 says "...that through death He might render powerless him who had the power of death, that is, the devil, and might free those who through fear of death were subject to slavery all their lives." Why would we choose to live a life of fear, a life of slavery. When we move through that fear, grasping tightly to God's hand, He will provide the way out. He will give us a spirit of courage, strength, and hope.

Run Rabbit Run

We all know the Chris Tomlin song, "I Will Follow." The chorus is simple, "Where you go, I'll go. Where you stay, I'll stay. When you move, I'll move. I will follow you." Such a great song taken from the words of Ruth, isn't it? It's easy to follow someone when their moving. It's the rest that is difficult.

Rabbits continually show me that there are two ways to react to fear – fight or flight. We know that. I guess that's why I love these rabbits. You see, I get up early before the sun to get my workout in. From spring to fall there are rabbits out and about. The front yards of neighbors and common area fields throughout my neighborhood are the morning feeding grounds for these sweet rabbits. You see the difference between the young, middle aged, and older rabbits.

As I run by, there are three reactions I could see. The first is the rabbit running away from me. I usually laugh at that rabbit because I have no chance of catching it. The second is the rabbit taking a hop or two and pausing. This rabbit usually scares me. I typically didn't see it there to begin with. It probably would've been better to just stay put. The third is that they don't move at all. You know these rabbits are older, seasoned rabbits. They know that I am too slow and uninterested in chasing around a rabbit at the wee early morning hours.

We've already talked about fear of failure. It traps you. You don't move. But many times we fear other options in life. Sometimes we fear being stuck at the dead end job and feel the need to jump ship. Other times we don't want to be considered a one trick pony, so we try new things. There are plenty of times that our life is filled with fear because we don't seem to be moving forward. Maybe that is there to motivate us or open our eyes, but it doesn't mean we need to run away.

See, just as fear of failure puts us into a frozen state of life, fear of the unknown can make us jump. One of my favorite verses in the Bible is Psalm 46:10. I'm sure many of you know it, or at least the first part. "Be still and know that I am God." You know that. Okay. Be still. Wait upon the Lord. We hear these things all the time because sometimes we just need to sit and wait. But when we wait, we aren't supposed to just settle in, we need to pray and seek His face. There may be something that you need to walk away from, but you might have to wait for His timing. Being still is one of the hardest things to do. In our society when something isn't exactly what we want, we are taught to change it, leave it, make it what we want. Yes, let's fight for what we want!

Or, we can go through the tough time that we are supposed to go through. We can deal with what we need to, which will usually make us stronger and better people for it. As much as I love to read "Be still and know that I am God," I love the rest of the verse.

Let's put it all together. "Be still and know that I am God. I will be exalted among the nations. I will be exalted in all the earth!" What? Get this. Please. Do not miss these words. We can be, nay, must be still. We must know the great I am, God almighty. If you stop and meditate on this verse, do not miss out on the end. "I will be exalted among the nations. I will be exalted in all the earth." Do you think that your fears are outside of the reach of the God that will be exalted above every nation on this earth? My heart gains strength in knowing that He will be exalted. He is exalted. He is the God of all. If He wants me to be still in a situation, wait for the right answer, then in my next move, I will be still.

The other morning I walked through the neighborhood. There was a sweet bunny waiting on the grass. He watched me pass on my side of the road. His one large eye followed me, but his body stayed still. His experience has shown him that I am not a threat to him. As I approached, I saw a black cat inching closer, inspecting the rabbit carefully. Once I had passed behind him completely, he picked up on the cat and bounded off to safety in the opposite direction. I walked and thought. I wondered if he would see the cat in time or if I would have to chase him away. I marveled at his intellect and ability to judge which time to stay and which time to run. I knew his fear was there, his gaze never left me.

I long to be like that rabbit. I long to know when to just stay. Where He goes, I'll go. Where He stays, I hope to stay. We can't let fear dictate where we go. Sometimes we just need to stay and watch.

Take a Swing at the Bride...

There is one visual that my pastor shares regularly: If you take a swing at the bride, you've taken a swing at the groom. What a thought. I was recently on the wrong side of a heated conversation. When I called my husband, who was on his way to where I was already, his response was, "He's lucky I wasn't there." If you knew my husband you would smile. In our relationship I am the fighter, while he is the peace keeper, think it out, let's not jump into this and keep calm guy. But the moment that a man came at me, he became a fighter. How much greater is that intensity with God for His church?

We quote Romans 8:31 everywhere, don't we? Chris Tomlin sang it, "If God is for us, who can be against us?" Amen! But then life gets going and we sort of forget that tidbit. Something comes against us and we lose our cool. We get flustered, frustrated, angry, and upset. We scream, cry, run away, and fight. What if we stopped and remembered who was fighting on our side?

Years ago, I entered a situation where I felt attacked on a regular basis. Wisdom from another Christian seeped into my life, and I hope it seeps into yours. They said, "Are you sure that they are attacking you? Maybe this non-Christian is attacking you for the Holy Spirit within you, not the flesh you're in." Woah. Stop for a second and think about that. When the world attacks us, how often is it that they are attacking the one within us, not us? They are attacking the bride. Don't you think the groom will handle it? It was at that time that I went into the KJV Bible and pulled out the "'Vengeance is mine,' thus saieth the Lord." Yes! That's it! Get them, God! They are attacking me, and therefore, you! Let them have it!

Do you hear the crickets? I did. God didn't take vengeance on them. I wanted immediate punishment. I wanted them to grovel at my feet and beg forgiveness. Never happened. Still waiting on that apology. The truth of it is, it will never come. I'll be waiting a long time. So what happened? Was God not faithful? It just isn't fair. He let me down. Once again, wisdom came to me, but this time from listening to God as I cried out for answers. It isn't time, yet. Just like I sinned and needed forgiveness and for God to rescue me, so did this individual. God wants this person to run into His arms just as much as He wanted me to.

Sometimes we are attacked by other Christians. That can be hard. There is much prayer that is needed during that time. Someone is in the wrong. Our pride says it's them, but we need to search our hearts. Is there something that caused the attack? Perhaps it is just jealousy. They see something in you that they want. Maybe you two had a fight, well then that's obvious. Often it is a misunderstanding. Remember, Satan wants to create rifts within the church. Here's the deal, you may need to humble yourself and apologize, even if you know you aren't wrong.

So where do we go from here? We need to keep moving forward. We pray for the people who persecute us as Jesus teaches in the sermon on the mount. We love those people, despite actions and words against you. Feeling wronged still? Look, I get it. I just don't get why that person treats me like that and I can't believe so-and-so said that. Ready for some guilt? "When they hurled their insults at him, he did not retaliate; when he suffered, he made no threats. Instead, he entrusted himself to him who judges justly." 1 Peter 2:23. Oh yeah. Jesus was hated. He was hated and crucified for being him. He went through more in three years of ministry on earth than most of us go through in a lifetime. And here we are whining that someone got in our face.

One thing I learned quickly was to hold my tongue. I never know what is going on with the other person. I don't know if they just had a bad day, lost a loved one, lost a job, or if they are just a jerk. But who am I to judge? Jesus entrusted himself to the one who will judge all justly. This little bit that I keep with me has saved me from some bad situations getting worse.

My son was picked on at school this past year. After a rough day, I asked him why he didn't fight back. It was the most calm response I have ever received from him. He looked at me and said, "I just didn't want to." And in an instant I realized how godly my six year old was. He knew there was no reason to fight back. I knew, when I looked in his eyes, that God was with him fighting for him in a different way. And he would make more of an impact without fighting back. It was a few weeks after that that I had my confrontation with the belligerent person I spoke of earlier. And as he got in my face, I took the words and let them go. I didn't respond besides the counselor approved, "I hear what you're saying. I understand. Okay." In my heart I heard the words my son spoke. I didn't feel like fighting. We don't always have to get in the ring. God has us in our hands. He will finish the fight in His own way.

Truth Hurts

Honesty has gotten a bad rap lately. I think I know why. Jesus said, "I am the truth, and the truth will set you free." From that time on, Satan has decided to trick people into thinking the truth is bad. We have to "sugar coat" things when we speak to others. We have to approach with a certain demeanor. If we are just flat out honest, well, we're blunt. We're hurtful.

Why is that? Why can't we just be honest to each other? When I was in middle school, someone taught me this little gag. You hit someone with a Bible. When they say "ow," you respond with, "Truth hurts!" Okay, I know it's lame. You don't have to tell me. But I think about it all the time. My beloved pastor repeats this phrase all the time when discussing the gospel: The gospel is offensive, we don't have to be. Well there it is. The gospel is the truth. And the gospel is offensive. Why? Because people don't want to hear that what they are doing, believing, or saying, is wrong. That's why truth is offensive. That's why honesty is frowned up.

People don't like it when you tell them the truth unless it is something sweet and pleasant. We all know when a wife asks her husband, "How do I look?" the response is supposed to be, "Perfect!"

When she asks, "Does my butt look big?" the answer is, "No way." Not in my house. I would rather have my husband tell me that I look like I got hit by a Mack truck if it's the truth. Why would I want to look horrible and leave the house? In our house we are honest. Truth reigns supreme.

The problem lies in this: nobody likes you when you're honest. Even if it's good honest, people won't like it. People like secrecy these days, and yet, we love Facebook and Twitter, Snapchat, and whatever else the next thing will be. We want to share our world, but only what we like about it. You know you see it all. We post the happy pictures with kids, except it was the hardest day with those little buggers. Some people have begun posting the bad pictures as well. That's sweet. But really, it's honest. People are finally posting pictures of the truth. Even people that have been transparent on Facebook receive the brutality of honesty. People roll their eyes, snort, and make comments (whether posted or not) about how that person is "whining" again or "just trying to get attention." When you're honest, nobody likes you. It's just how it is.

So when we look back at Scripture and we see what Jesus told his disciples, we see more truth. He tells them flat out, people won't like you. People will hate you, just as people hated Him. We know that applies to us today. We know that following Christ will cause the world to hate us. Most of us are okay with it, in general. Let me ask you this – when did we decide what the world can hate us for and what they can't? It seems okay for the world to hate us because we love Jesus. Somehow, somewhere, some point in time, people decided it was not okay to be disliked for telling the truth. Feelings are hurt. It's all about our emotions. I can honestly say this: My long term emotional struggles would have been far better if people had told me the truth.

Let's take it back to grade school. There's a bully. He picks on the kid next to him. What do we do? We punish the bully. We talk to the kids. Do we tell them the truth? I'll answer that one, I sure did. When my son was being picked on by a kid in his class for being "little" I told him the truth. That kid is jealous. He is jealous that you skipped kindergarten. He's jealous that you're smarter than him. He's jealous that you're better behaved and get rewarded for your behavior. I didn't lie to my son and tell him that the boy was playing or being silly. I didn't tell him that the boy probably didn't know what to say. I told him the truth. Ya know what? My son walked into school the next day with confidence – not cockiness. He knew that the reason he was picked on was because the other kid was jealous. Isn't that what most bullies are? Jealous?

Why do we cover things up and try to hide the truth. Jesus said in Matthew, "nor does anyone light a lamp and put it under a basket, but on the lamp stand, and it gives light to all who are in the house." The truth may not be what you or others want to hear, but shouldn't it be said?

People say I'm rough around the edges and blunt. Truth is, I'm just honest and people aren't used to it. I deliver the truth as best as I can to be helpful, not hurtful. The truth doesn't have to be condescending, rude, or judgmental. Speak with grace as seasoned with salt. We should be building up and edifying. We can do that with honesty.

Behold, I Stand and Knock

Christians, do we know the Scripture by now? "Behold, I stand at the door and knock." (Rev. 3:20) Beautiful. Simple. We hear this and know that for us to receive the grace of God and a change of heart we must open the door and allow Jesus in. I've adopted the statement my pastor repeats, "He is a gentleman. Jesus is not going to kick down the door." It's the truth. We have free will. We have choices. We make the decision about Jesus and our hearts on our own.

So here's what I want to get at. He is always at the door waiting. Picture it, you're in the middle of something and the door bell rings. First thought is, "Who's that?" or "What now?" Then you answer the door. You shoo them away, you let them in, you welcome them in, or you don't even open the door. We're taught in the time of salvation that He knocks, we open and He comes to live in our hearts and we're hunky dorey.

Now I am not saying that we lose our salvation. We are sealed in the Holy Spirit for the day of redemption (Eph. 1:13). However, I am going to take some creative liberties with the visual of Jesus coming in to love in our hearts. You know what it's like when you're living with someone that you love dearly, but sometimes you just want them out of the house. You want some alone time, or whatever. I think that we too often send Jesus out to pick up a jug of milk so we can do something we know He might not approve of. Okay, well, maybe I'm the only one who does that.

Let's take this a little further. We give him residency. We allow Him in, but shouldn't we be welcoming Him in? My favorite thing to see is when my kids know that their grandparents are coming over. You can picture it; the ceaseless questions about time, the constant checking the windows for a familiar car to come, the waiting on the front porch or sidewalk to be there with a smile for their loved ones. And what happens? They meet them at the car with open arms and walk them to the house.

Why don't we do that with God? We should be inviting Him in with open arms. I see it all over the place. I see it in myself all the time. "Hey, Jesus! What's up, man? You good? You look good." Then I think. Yeah, it's good having him here. And then we keep going with life. We fill our days with work, play, and other people. We forget He's there sometimes. Sometimes we leave him behind. "Hey, Jesus, if you want to hang here it's cool. Throw on the 700 club or something. I'm heading out with these people. I'm probably going to say or do something stupid... so... ya know..."

We need to do better. I need to do better. I need to invite Him in to more. One area I stay on top of, I feel I do anyway, is parenting. When it comes to the "mom" me, I invite Jesus into my parenting. I want my kids to not just enjoy going to church. I want my kids to live a life that reflects my walk, their father's walk, and grandparents of generations past. I want Jesus embedded in their lives that they love so fiercely that people will live in awe and wonder of what they do and HOW they do it.

I just wish I invited Jesus into everything else that way. My kids do Bible studies and memory verses. We pray constantly. But what about when I go out shopping? Am I driving with grace? (Don't bother holding it in, I'm laughing at that one too.) Can't we all do a little more to step up our game? Don't just open the door. Invite him in. Take him with you. Be glad he came.

Are We in the Boat or on the Land?

One of my favorite passages in the Bible is Luke 5:1-11. There's so much depth in just one paragraph.

We start with the enormity of the crowd and their desire for Jesus that they are pushing and shoving. If you're like me you've been to a concert before. If not, I hope you can imagine it. With many young adults, the goal is to get as close to the stage as possible. How does one do that? They get there early and lay claim to the fence that divides them from the stage, or they inch their way up through the crowd. Some inchers are nice about it. An open space to the right and they slip in, constantly gliding into any 6x12 inch space someone has left themselves for comfort. Others are more abrasive. They plow their way through pushing, using elbows, stepping on the smaller attendees. This is followed up by someone holding ground. The crowd gets upset. Pushing ensues. I have this concert like visual in my mind when I read this passage. I picture men sliding into open areas and men bulldozing their way to the front with arrogance. Jesus doesn't have a fence. He doesn't have security. There is no stage for Him. So he looks around and hops in an unattended boat and asks the owner of the boat to push it out a bit.

This part always gets interesting to me. I was once taught that Jesus would prefer to speak to a large crowd from a boat. Why? The water would help project his voice back to the crowd. It would put less of a strain on him. So it kind of is like this boat is his stage and the water his microphone. Jesus in the start of his ministry was the Justin Bieber of his time. (Don't murder me for that reference.) However, he was followed by highly devoted people, but the majority of those around him were actually against him. Crowds flocked to him, followed him. They would have made robes with his face and name on them, if they could. And people knew what he was speaking about, and then wondered if they too liked him, kind of like if you hear a Bieber song and enjoy it then realize who is singing it.

So now that I've thrown a little background to the opening of the passage, let me get into my revelation within it. Most people, myself included, focus on verses 10 and 11, "Jesus said to Simon, "Do not fear, from now on you will be catching men.' When they had brought their boats to land, they left everything and followed him." I bet most of you just nodded right along with that. Yup, drop everything and go catch men for Jesus. Got it.

The second most famous part is verses 4-7. Jesus tells Peter to put his net in and though they had caught nothing all night, Peter does so. They haul in so many fish the boat starts to sink. We learn our lesson on faith and putting action to God's words. What a rich paragraph this is.

But my spiritual epiphany runs the course around these two parts. I don't want to look at a specific verse per say. I don't need to dissect anything. I want to see the whole picture.

Jesus, being bombarded by an eager crowd, steps into a boat to speak to them. After he has taught the word of God to the crowd, He addresses Peter and his net. He's working on two sets of people in two distinct ways. I can see how Jesus continues to work in this way today. I think people often get jealous of the other at various points in their lives, but none the less God works both ways each day.

You see, sometimes we're the crowd. Jesus gets into His boat and he teaches us a lesson. From there it's our job to go out into the world and apply the lesson into our everyday lives. That can be hard. Sometimes we forget what he is teaching us. Sometimes we ignore what he spoke. Being in the crowd while he teaches us can often feel like he wasn't actually speaking directly to us. That can be difficult to understand and follow through with. It's easy to be jealous of the Simon Peters on the boat with Jesus.

That's the second way God is working in us. After letting out his teaching to the crowd he turns to us and says, "You, do this." Having the task given to us can be easier than trying to decipher what to do like the crowd. He told a fisherman to put his net into the Lake of Gennesaret. It was the same lake this guy fished on all night. It's not some big deal to ask a fisherman to fish. But Peter doesn't respond with, "Sure, okay, sounds good Jesus." Nope. Peter basically says, "We did this all night and failed. What makes you think it will work now?" I bet he was a little cocky when he said he would do it, like a *This isn't going to work, but whatever,* moment. So he throws the net. It's hard to throw that net. It's hard to hear God speak to you directly and say, "do this," and actually follow up and do it.

Now I'm sure it was a little different for Peter. Jesus was in his boat. Peter didn't have that nervous butterfly feeling in his belly that says, "Maybe I wasn't hearing God's voice." How amazing would that be for Jesus to sit in the car with us and say, "You know what you need to do…"? Could you just imagine the physical, pre-up-to-heaven-at-the-right-hand-of-our-Father Jesus sitting with us and telling us what to do? I bet we would do whatever He said.

Let's get away from that daydream and back to the topic. God is speaking to us. In the crowds Jesus often spoke in parables. Why? He explains that those who understand the parables are his brothers and sisters. Sometimes when God tells us to do something through teaching, it still feels like we're getting a parable. Maybe it's just me, but when I leave a convicting sermon I start with an exact idea of what God meant, but then I wonder. "Is it that? Maybe he meant this. Should I really share that word with that person? Maybe I'm just supposed to pray over them." If only God would text us what He wants to teach us, but there's no syllabus for a walk with God.

It's just as hard when we get that strong, clear voice spoken to us. Doors open and we're supposed to walk through. That can't be too hard, right? But it is. Many times when we are told what to do, someone else was told too. Do you think a crowd of followers just up and left after Jesus taught? Doubtful. Then He performs a little fish miracle. Have they left now? Not likely. And Jesus tells Simon, James and John to leave it all behind. I bet the crowd heard that too. You know what I'm talking about too. There's someone you know who is not working in their God given talents and gifts. It's slowly killing them, but they need the money to survive. Last time I checked, when we walk with God on His plan, He provides what we need. So when you receive that direct instruction from God, it can be hard to follow it. There's a good chance what you're told is not logical. If it were, it wouldn't require faith, and you probably would have done it already.

So if you ask me if I would rather be in the crowd when he teaches, or in the boat with his direct words, I can't tell you which I want to be. I think it depends on my stage of life and what the lessons and directions are. Regardless of which way God is speaking to me, I know that my faith will be put to the test. If I pass that test I don't care if I was in the crowd or on the boat. Because at the end of the day, I am thankful for a God that speaks to me through teaching and direction. Aren't you?

Proverbs 31 Woman

Men, you may be tempted to skip over this one, but I assure you it has a use for you too. If you ever plan on getting married, if you may ever have a daughter, or if you are already there with either or both of those, than you get a little insight as to what has been taught to us girls growing up in the church.

Let me begin with the basics. The 31st chapter of Proverbs is the last one. The first nine verses are titles "The Words of Lemuel" which are words his mother taught him, according to the first verse. Then at verse 10 the switch comes in. He writes about the drinking of kings and then rapidly changes the thought process to a worthy woman. I don't know about you, but I think it interesting to see the words about a ruler not having a heavy drink followed by how to find a worthy wife. But I digress. The next 21 verses show us what a worthy woman looks like.

I'd like to start with the verse that is drilled into the heads of young women in our girls only Bible study groups. "Charm is deceitful and beauty is vain, but a woman who fears the Lord is to be praised." It's no wonder this is the verse that is focused on. It teaches both women and men what the purpose of life truly is. Life isn't about the outward appearance or charming others into liking you. Life is about fearing the Lord above. There is nothing I can possibly disagree with in this verse. However, I struggle with the issue that this is the only part of the scripture that is continually focused on.

So now we can dive into the rest of the chapter, can't we? Within the beginning we learn that we are about to find someone worth more than jewels. There is trust from her husband. I know firsthand what that does for a woman. My husband trusts me in every aspect of our lives. He believes in me and trusts that I will do well with whatever I am led to do. So why does the Proverbs 31 woman gain the trust of her husband? Let's take a look.

She does her husband good. She looks for wool and flax. She works with her hands with delight. She brings her food from afar, and rises while it is night to feed her household. She buys a field after consideration and plants vincyard. She makes coverings for herself. She makes linen garments and sells them, and supplies belts to the tradesmen. All of these could be summed up in the 27th verse: She looks well to the ways of her household, and does not eat the bread of idleness.

Has anyone ever read those verses from start to finish and just felt exhausted? I sure do. I read these verses and see that the description of a "Worthy Woman" is that of a woman that works incredibly hard. She wakes up early and prepares food for her household. She works with seeds, linens, and in fields. This woman doesn't sit down and chat it up with her girlfriends. There are no coffee breaks with the moms' morning out group. No, this woman works from before the sun rises until the end of the day. Her husband trusts her because she is always doing something productive for her family. The final verse of the chapter says, "Give her the product of her hands, and let her works praise her in the gates." What else could I say about her work?

Verse 17 says, "She girds herself with strength and makes her arms strong." I can't tell you how much I love this verse. It's placed right between planting a vineyard with her earnings and knowing that she is doing well because the lamp does not go out at night. She has plenty of oil for her lamps. She has worked and earned it, and that is why she girds herself with strength. A worthy woman according to the book of Proverbs is a woman that is strong. It isn't her voice that is strong, it's her arms, her body, her mind. She makes herself strong for the work she does and from the work she had done. This woman was still submissive to her husband – she does him good and not evil, she feeds him, clothes him – but that didn't make her weak. Strong women have been given a bad name through the past. Why? Women, don't you want to be strong? Men, don't you want a strong woman in your corner versus a weak one? Contemplate that one for a moment. Think about all the gender role issues you've been taught. Roll it around for a bit.

Along with the fear of the Lord, business sense, and strength, the worthy woman is wise, generous, and kind. Verse 26 says, "She opens her mouth in wisdom, and the teaching of kindness is on her tongue." That's a woman to stand near and learn from. Too many people speak for the sake of the nothing. A woman that gives insights, wisdom, and kindness when she speaks is a woman that needs to be listened to. And she doesn't just speak about kindness, she also demonstrates it. "She extends her hand to the poor, and she stretches out her hands to the needy." This is a woman who practices what she preaches. Perhaps it's where I am in life, but I feel we do not see as much help to the needy and poor as we need to see. If we are women like this, we should be extending our hands. Men, do you encourage the women in your life to do so?

It's interesting to really dive into these verses and see all the things that make a woman worthy. How much has society influenced our teaching of this passage? How many times have lessons been built around a woman choosing to lay aside her beauty? Read these verses. Study them. See the amazing things, countless things that the worthy woman does in the day.

Empty Vessels

Throughout the Old and New Testament we see the reference to how we are mere lumps of clay that need to be worked by the Potter. It's beautifully poetic. It reaches us on so many levels. Some clay is used for noble activity, while other for common. It gives us a place. We are all pieces of God's artwork ready to be used.

The problem with that today is that people have too many pieces of pottery on display and we don't understand their functions. Back in the wonderful 1990's a band called Jars of Clay came out. Christian teens were stoked. A band that claims Christ first and foremost had crossed into the other side, the secular world of music. And they did so with a Christian song, no less, Flood. That led to many of us learning the name of the band had a biblical reference.

I heard so much about clay and the vessels we become. God has the ability to mold us however He sees fit and however many times he needs to. So here we are. God has worked us into this vessel. There is a lump of clay turned into a jar. Now what?

Some of us have gotten some cracks along the way. When we are poured into, we lose some of what was poured into us. Isn't that how it seems? We sit in church, Bible study, our quiet times, we get and get and get, and yet, something is missing. Something isn't sinking in. We feel like we're missing God. But those holes and cracks can be patched. And they will. With prayer, and God, we can have that clay patched on and become a vessel that can be used. That's where we want to be. We need to be useful clay vessels.

You know I have to ask a follow up. What happens to water when it sits? Stagnant water is nasty. Mold and muck take over. Stagnant water is no good. It is useless. So we become a vessel that is useful, and then we hold onto water. Not for long, I hope. I think that's why I love the name Jars of Clay so much. It gives me that visual. That jar is a tool. The water goes in, the water gets poured out. It can't just hold the water. We are meant for so much more than taking in God's word and holding it tight. We have to use it. If we are living for God, we must also work for Him.

Be someone that takes in and pours out to others. That could look like a variety of things. It might mean that we are to love on someone or pray for them. It might mean sharing a word that God has given us. Sometimes that can be easy. Many times it's difficult. We have that awkward feeling, like we aren't good enough to be that person for them, or we don't know them. But when we remember that our battle is not with flesh and blood (Eph. 6:12) we can approach those around us and be more usable. The best part about being a vessel that is usable, is that once you begin the process of allowing yourself to be used, you will be used even more. So we find ourselves being poured into more and pouring out more. It's almost like your favorite coffee cup. It starts as being a mug you like, but as life moves on that mug moves with you. The pictures fade. The cup acquires stains. And each time you use it, you fall in love with it more and keep it in the front of the cabinet each time it's washed. Soon even the neighbors know what your favorite coffee cup looks like.

If we aren't willing to be used, what will happen to those around us? I love the references in Jeremiah and Isaiah to the potter and the clay – they ask us, can the clay tell the potter what it wants to become? So often, God is crafting us to be someone that we think just isn't right. So we keep trying to fit ourselves into a different mold. When we get ourselves in line with God, we can feel him pushing and guiding us into the vessel that he desires us to be. The next step is getting into being used in that capacity. We have to release the fear and doubt and do what God calls us. Just as people have had that impact on you, or maybe there was a need that wasn't met in you, that is what you must step into.

If you're a bowl, be a bowl. If you're a pitcher, be a pitcher. If you are still being crafted, let the potter shape you, and be grateful for every day of the process.

Christian Karma

Okay, I'm going to be honest here. What is going on with my Christian Facebook friends these days? I am struggling to understand some of the things they say. I'm going to give you my top three "What?" phrases, links, etc. that I just cannot get past. If I offend you I want you to know, I am not sorry. This might just be what you need to read. This list is not in any specific order.

Number 1: Christian Karma – "It's okay, what goes around comes around. Karma baby."

No. That isn't what happens, and you should know that if you are following Christ. Karma is actually from Hinduism and Buddhism. It is the sum of a person's actions in this and previous lives which will then decide what their future life will be. So when you say, "what goes around comes around," you're really saying, "they were a jerk to me yesterday so when they die they will become and earthworm."

Let's get away from why this whole Christian Karma thing is wrong, and make some corrections to the thinking. God blesses the least, that isn't Karma, that is grace, benevolence, love. Christians will struggle for the sake of Christ. That doesn't mean that someone else is going to get theirs later on because they persecuted you. What it does mean is that God sees and knows your suffering and will offer peace and a heavenly retribution at the end of times. We know from Psalms that God does indeed fight for us. So at the very least, we can say, "God will take care of my enemies." But to think that God and Karma are teaming up to beat up that guy who cut you off in the Wal-Mart parking lot? No. I'm pretty sure the God of all is not sitting with a multi-armed elephant telling it what to make us when we pass. But you if think so, you are not a follower of Christ.

Number 2: Good Vibes and Good Thoughts

This one I see far too often. It's finals time, a new job opportunity, or a doctor's appointment and here are people dropping it on Facebook. "Hey guys could you pray, send good vibes or good thoughts for me…" Oh good heavens people. I've actually read on one person's post, "whichever you do…" At least that person didn't claim Christianity. However, when a youth pastor "friend" posted that he was worried about his final and asked for prayers, good vibes and good thoughts I was about to lose it. At least the non-Christian was right. You have to pick one. Either you believe in the power of prayer or you don't. Plain and simple.

Don't start meshing together the things of God and the things of the world. When you claim Christ, then you must do so in an all or nothing way. You are either for God or against him. Remember in Revelation 3:15-16, Jesus speaks to the church of Laodicea saying that because they are neither hot nor cold, they would be spit out from His mouth. You have to choose, one way or the other. There's no dancing between the two. Here, let me send you some vibes. Got 'em? Feeling better? How about my thoughts. Oh, please. How often did you think of that classmate in middle school that you wanted to date? You can think something about someone all day and night, doesn't mean anything is going to happen. We're too worried about offending those that don't pray, but if you believe in Christ, you must believe in prayer. Prayer will do more than good vibes or happy thoughts could ever do. And isn't it better to offend someone who doesn't believe than offend God?

Number 3: What's your sign?

Okay, guys. Seriously? Do we need a history lesson in horoscopes, signs, and other paganistic items? When I see a Christian post about their horoscope I really have to wonder- did they do it as a joke? But then I stop and think, how would they have known to post it if they hadn't looked it up? I'm sorry (not really) but if you believe in an Almighty God that loves you and cares about you on a day to day basis, then why in the world do you look to what the alignment of the stars says based on your birthday? Someone help me out with this one because I just don't get it. Horoscopes in general make no sense. To see a Christian repeatedly post their horoscope on Facebook makes me wonder what that person is thinking. When people ask me my sign, I answer a cross. That's the only sign I need.

So maybe right now you are a little offended by my statements and accusations. That's fine with me. You grab your Bible. I'll grab mine. Let's see who ends up where. I'll take standing up for God's truth every time. I do hope, however, that maybe you are convicted by your use of these. Maybe it's time for you to sit down with that Bible and read up about God. Discover who He is. Know the times He is there for us, on our side, speaking on our behalf. Know when Christ is interceding for us before God. Know that our plans are laid out by the Sovereign One, not the stars he placed in the sky.

Yeast Rolls

This is an old piece I wrote while flying back from a trip to Las Vegas. Before you get any ideas, let me give you some back story. My father wanted to take a trip before my brother got married that was just the four of us. Well, my brother and his fiancé pushed the wedding up and so my mother, father and I went to Las Vegas for a family trip. I was twenty, and a third wheel. Anyway, because of the situation, I was able to write this while flying back to Providence (where I would then have to drive back to Charleston):

A lot of thinking lately. A lot of bad choices. A time of reflection, contemplation, consideration, and much more. First of all, how amazing is our God? As I have been listening to the new Chris Tomlin (now quite old, don't judge me) I can't help but be swept away by the humbling lyrics. Words like, "indescribable," "great," "awesome," "unfailing," "enough," etc., seem to continually describe the God of all creation. And I am trying to make a habit of not just singing the well placed words on rhythms, but meaning what is said. Don't sing because the song is pretty, or it makes you feel good, but sing because you mean it and have decided to spend your time praising the King of all that is and is to come!

As I ventured out to a cliff/overhang in the Grand Canyon, I couldn't help but think, "Wow! How awesome is our God? He created this. He knew that this canyon was going to be shaped just as it is." God knew that one day I would be on that piece of rock in the midst of His creation watching eagles soar across the canyon while the sun set. He is truly amazing!

He has shown His majesty in so many ways that I wonder now: How many times and how many ways is God continually trying to reveal His majesty, glory, and power to us and we turn and ignore it all? He is constantly showing His glory in His creations. How often do we miss that?! It is one of the reasons why I enjoy being outside so often. But where else do I miss Him? Maybe starting conversations. Maybe helping someone. Or even, dare I say it, turning off the television!

I believe it is time for R^2 - Revival and Revolution. "If God is on our side, who can be against us?" So why do we, I, sit and wait. Is there not spiritual warfare now? Why wait for a degree? Why wait for a position in the church? You are the church. Get up and go. What holds us back? As I have a second thought process going on, I realize that that is the answer to my question. I recently told a friend of my insecurities, low self esteem, and things that go along with that. It is that very thing that keeps me from what I should be doing. Paul says in Romans- I do the things I wish I did not do and do not do the things I should or want to do. Why is this? It is because not all has been given over to God. We are quenching the Holy Spirit, are we not? He has provided power. A spirit of power and not of timidity

(Timothy). We have power when the Holy Spirit comes upon us (Acts 1:8). So it is us and our insecurities, fears, self righteous lives that keep us from the work of God. This brings me to my next point of writing for the evening.

My eyes have been opened to the selfish ways of man in the past week. Every Christian knows of the self centered world of every man, but it is my belief that we each choose to ignore it. Why? Because deep inside we know it is not just the non-Christian, but us as well. Christ says not to worry about the speck in your neighbor's eye when you have not taken the plank out of yours. Well, wake up Christians, we have misinterpreted this passage. It does not mean to ignore the situation, but to take out our planks! I suppose we assume if we are not worrying about our neighbor's speck than we are obeying Christ, but what about getting our own plank out?! Do we think Scripture is saying to let it go? I don't think so. The plank of all people, whether Christian or not, is pride. C.S. Lewis addresses this beautifully in "Mere Christianity." We forget to love our neighbor as ourselves.

While walking the Strip and interacting with different people I have seen how selfish they were. But then I asked, "Why do they seem so selfish?" That's when it hit me. They are selfish because they aren't doing what I would like them to do, or aren't doing it my way. How selfish am I? Here I am worrying about the self centeredness of "unbelievers" (a speck) while I am ignoring my own self centeredness (the big ole plank). I have noticed something, though. Since my eyes have been opened to the truth of our conceit, especially my own, I have seen a change. My demeanor has become different, softer. I feel God changing my view from what is best for me, or even what is most convenient for me, to what about others. I can only say it is God doing it and I can only ask that He continue in the never ending process. –end

Why did I throw this journal entry in? Honestly, I should separate it out and make different topics laid out, but I couldn't. I couldn't let go of that night on the plane. Sometimes when God pours out His word, He lays it on all at once. There are a couple of different topics. It jumps, yes. That is why I call it yeast rolls- so much buttery goodness in one piece. I hope that from the variety within this piece you grab a hold of something.

Room for Gray

In the Christian community it has always been said that there is black and white- no room for gray. However, I beg to differ. I wonder as I analyze all of this if it is truth from the Holy Spirit or just me being in a post modern time where traditions are challenged and the overall thought is that truth is relevant. Now please don't misinterpret me on this. I believe that truth is solid and does not change according for each person. Truth is not relative, it is absolute. But my wonder comes from if this line of thinking is my influence.

Anyway, I ask: Is there gray in the Christian world? Jesus says in Matthew that if you are not with Him you are against Him. That is black and white. No exceptions. You are either for or against, you can't be both. But on certain issues, can there be gray? Are we allowed to have gray? Should it be all black and white? In Romans 15 Paul discusses the issue of food and convictions related to the food. He talks about how one person's convictions may not be the same as others. Both are doing what they believe to be right in their worship and devotion to God.

Now my next question comes in how literal I should translate this passage. Was this written for the Romans and only for the Romans? Or was this a passage Paul wrote, inspired by the Holy Spirit, to reach the Roman believers and others as well, even today? I can interpret it for today's world. Alcohol. Some say it should never touch your lips. Why? It's wrong. It leads to bad things. I think the only Scripture I have found to combat drinking alcohol would be 1 Corinthians 6:9 about taking care of your body because it is the temple of the Holy Spirit living in you. This verse applies as we have found out how alcohol damages the body- liver, kidneys, brain cells. Other Christians would say that drinking is okay in moderation. "Scripture doesn't come out and say not to drink. It says not to become drunken with wine." "It doesn't affect the love I have for God." And, of course, my personal favorite justification of drinking, "Jesus turned water into wine." So is it okay to drink? What if the conviction is public drinking? It is okay to drink in the privacy of one's home, not for the thought of being judged, but to keep from being a stumbling block. Is this gray? It looks gray to me. Is there a right and a wrong? Is it all right? Each having their own conviction, as in Romans 15, was that just for Messianic Jews and early Christians with their food laws or does it apply to us to? This could be a stumbling block for others. If they don't agree with drinking alcohol, or maybe they think you have had more to drink than you have. One may argue that it is not their prerogative, but becoming a stumbling block to someone else can be a serious thing as well.

So let's look at the word "church". Now my belief is that we are the church, the body. It doesn't matter the building, the music, or the dress code, but let me use this word as it has been used in our culture for ages. Is going to church Sunday mornings the right thing to do? We often discuss the day and time to feel that we are above the judgmental claims of this issue. Does it have to be Sunday? Well, that is today's version of the Sabbath. But if we were to go by the book, we should be going to church on Saturday. So, okay, it doesn't matter. That's just what most churches do because of the celebration of Christ's resurrection which occurred on a Sunday. That is the traditional day we chose. So what about the time? For most churches, it is 11 am. Big churches may have multiple services, but usually always in there is an 11 am service. So why is this the holy time? It isn't. But when farming was the main source of nourishment, funds, and well, life, the daily chores- like milking Bessy- needed to be done and thus the service time was later in the morning so that the people could take care of what needed to be done. (We can dive into the fact that the church time was set around daily chores that were done on a Sunday in a different chapter- What would the Pharisees think?!)

Alright, we have handled the day and time like good modernistic thinking has taught us, so now we can go back to the question and answer the part that I want answered. Is "going to church" Sunday mornings the right thing to do? If I don't show up on a Sunday morning, am I wrong? The widow mother of three that needs to work on Sundays, is she wrong? What about house churches? Are they wrong? Scripture talks about the importance of corporate worship for the building up of the saints. Does that mean the only place I can get that is at "church"?

What about a ministry at the local high school? Does that count? Or maybe a Bible study that is done in a dorm from for 8 girls. Are these not corporate worship gatherings? So is there a right and wrong? Or is there gray?

It is my gut feeling that we are too stuck in the black and white Christian society. I believe there is a great deal of gray to be worked through. This gray, though, is not in everything. Sin is sin. All good things come from God. His grace is our only hope. But some are convicted by things others aren't. I believe this is one of the main reasons it is continually said that no one knows a man's heart but God. It is why we should not cast judgment on one another. There is black. There is white. There is gray. Isn't there?

Purposed Mistakes

I don't know if you're like me or not, but sometimes I think we make mistakes on purpose. It's odd. Perhaps it's just our struggle with life and frustrations. Maybe we're just bored.

Most of my life I have been jealous of the big converts. You know the ones; drugs, sex, alcohol, destitution, redemption, forgiveness, miraculous healing. Man, those people have a testimony don't they? What a story! The emotional roller coaster is too intense. I wish I had a radical change that would lead people to the cross. But I don't.

I was born and raised in the church. At the age of four I gave my life to Christ. I remember it clearly. I prayed during children's church with Miss Eve for Jesus to come into my heart and forgive me for all my sin. Then over the next few days and weeks it continued. I was terrified that ALL of my sins wouldn't be forgiven. What if I lied and forgot about it? Would he forgive that too? The answer is yes, but I didn't know that at the time. I mean, I was four. Over the course of my life I tried to play the good girl as best as I could. I had some bad moments, but overall I was straight edge. I was clean. No issues with me. Emotionally, I had a great deal of trauma that came out in my "bad girl" items, but I never got drunk, never smoked pot. I didn't have a big redemption story. That was probably because I was born and raised in the church. I always knew that God was watching and couldn't let myself go off the deep end.

As I got into college and on my own I realized I had a great deal more freedom. I had opportunities. I had a way to hide bad if I so chose. After years and years of the good being beaten into my head, I wondered what it would be like if I wasn't that way. So many people have had these crazy lives doing crazy things and make mistakes. Then they find Jesus and give it up. But for those of us that walk the straight and narrow (or at least try to), and have always had Jesus walking along side us, with the teachings buried deep within us, we sometimes long for the chance to go crazy. So we choose to make mistakes. We chose to date the guy that we know isn't a Christian because, well, who cares? We choose to go out and get drunk because, well, who will know? We choose to get high with our roommates because if they're doing it too, it can't be that bad. We have those choices laid out for us, if we want them.

I understand what Paul writes in Romans 6:1-2 "What shall we say then? Are we to continue in sin so that grace may increase? May it never be! How shall we who died to sin still live in it?" No matter how young or old we were when we found the Lord, we decided to die to sin. Paul tells us that our sin is covered by the grace of God through the blood of Christ. What a relief! When we confess our sins he is indeed faithful and just to forgive us. However, that doesn't give us a license to sin. When I was in high school I would go out with a guy on a Saturday and stay out until 2am. No, I wasn't sleeping with him, or anything like that. I might have a beer or two, though I knew I shouldn't. The next morning I would wake up and pray for forgiveness only to repeat the process the next weekend.

I was putting myself in situations that could have ended up far, far worse. I look back now and see how I was protected the entire time. Even in my adult life I wanted to screw up. I wanted to make mistakes. I wanted to do something that would really make a difference when I told people my story. Maybe you're in my shoes and you understand. Maybe you're the person I've been jealous of and you're screaming at me, "No! No! Don't make mistakes for the sake of making them! I have so many regrets!"

I think that is part one of the point of all this. We all have regrets. We all have guilt and shame. Maybe it's something considered "major" or not. God doesn't judge the level of our sins, we do that to cope and deal. Sin is sin. White lies are still lies. Impurity is still impurity. Spitting in the face of laws is still a disregard of rules set before us. At the end of the day, the Christian sitting next to you is dealing with the same feelings and emotions that you are, no matter which side you're on. The beauty of the cross is that the blood covers all sin. It takes no account of how big or small.

The second part is this: it isn't about us. My jealousy of a boring testimony left me with feelings of resentment towards God. Why didn't I get to have a crazy life? No, I had to keep being good because I knew the God of all creation and his expectations for his children. Why didn't I get to have a testimony that is big and revolutionary? I'm just the consistent same ole same ole here in the church girl. How selfish a thought?! God allowed me to find him at a young age. He protected me and kept me out of harm's way even when I wanted to be stupid. That feeling of guilt, that God was there with me watching me, not allowing me to dive into the deep end, was his way of keeping me with Him. Okay, sure, I made some mistakes, most of which knowingly. My God's grace covers even my sin when I do it on purpose, once I've repented truly.

My focus has been on me, my testimony, my lack of a dramatic change. The focus should be on Christ. I shouldn't downplay my testimony because I wasn't a dancer on the Las Vegas Strip. I should be willing to stand up for the testimony that God gave me. He rescued me. He continued to keep me from myself. Shall I continue to make mistakes on purpose to experience His grace? May it never be! I will happily walk with His grace from glory to glory and pray that those who had a similar upbringing won't make purposeful mistakes like I did.

Preach Preacha'

When I began this piece, it was indeed a little older than this publishing. I wrote this in 2005, and I think you can see that, but it still applies to today. So go with it. Take a trip down memory lane before you get into the heart of it.

You never know what you have until it's gone. Hurricane Katrina swept through the south destroying everything in her path. People now know what they have. But that is what we care about. I have a different thought. Christ. We base our world on what we have, but do we have Christ? Many who do have Christ are still focused on materials. Christians worry about their house, car, clothes, anything and everything.

We should be the first ones to give all we have to the victims of Katrina. And we will, I hope. We will give a donation – money, food, water. But will we give Christ? Will we be the ones to say, and live, that it is not what is in this world that matters, but heavenly treasures. We sing praise songs that say, "Blessed be the name of the Lord" in suffering, in the desert, in the good and bad times. We sing that though God will give and take away we will bless His holy name. But do we really do that? Do we bless God in hard times? Do we thank Him for taking things or even people away? Not often, if ever. Too many times we are stuck on our selfish ambition to gain, gain, gain, that we curse God when something is taken away. We are quick to say "All things work for the good of those who believe," but behind the words of our mouths is "Why did you have to do that God?! I liked that. It made me happy! I'm comfortable and I need that in my life!" Hello? Is God not bigger than your "need?" His is all you need! Just Him.

Did David have an accountability group when he was a shepherd boy? Did Moses have a mentor? Did Esther go to the same church every Sunday, sit in the same spot, and talk to the same people? All those things are good, but they are not what we need to focus on. God should be so much of a need in our lives that we should be in withdrawal without him.

We are comfortable Christians. I know everyone says that. And everyone tries to combat the comfort, but do we? Are you doing something that makes you uncomfortable? Are you being taken out of the same ministry position you've been in for three years? Have you helped the same group of people only? Every day you should feel uncomfortable at least once. Each day should bring you to some place you don't like. You're thinking why? Why every day? Why is this so important?

I'll tell you why. We are called to be in the world and not of it. If we go through a whole day and not feel a bit of discomfort we may be molding into the world too much. If we have comfort, we feel okay. We can handle life. We don't need God. Oops, did I say that? When we feel we can handle our life we tell God, "I don't need you." In case you missed this from previous pages, God is the one we need. Yet, we are willing to tell him we don't need him. HA! What we are is comfortable. I'm happy for Hurricane Katrina. It might just be a wake-up call. Those who don't know Christ can see how things are "here today, gone tomorrow," but God is always here. For those who call themselves followers of Christ, this pushes their faith. Those who lost what they have, will they bless his holy name? Those who weren't directly affected, will they give up their comforts for another? You never know what you've gone until it's gone. Good news is – God will never be gone.

Alarm Clock

The face of American Christians is the look of shock. It seems like everywhere I look Christians just can't believe what is happening in the world. Why? Why are you so appalled? So you're telling me that in a fallen and depraved world non-Christians are engaging in sinful activity? Moses must be rolling over in his grave! Mostly because of your naivety and lack of spiritual maturity. Really people? Why do we cause such drama every time non-Christians act like non-Christians? Stop acting like hormonal adolescents and grow up! Yes, even in this country, that you're convinced is a Christian nation, but has never been and probably never will be, there are non believers who will act in sinful manners. I'm sorry to be blunt, but someone had to tell it to you straight. We cannot keep holding non believers to Biblical standards. So stop being surprised by their actions.

Today, the world is experiencing many acts of terrorism. Death tolls are higher and higher. I see my Christian brothers and sisters getting in their two cents on what to do. They focus on their life here in the great US of A and tell the rest of us what it is we should be doing. The problem with that is that they aren't telling me to do what Christ told me to do. Therefore, I can't stand with them. I wonder how many of my politically active Christian friends are reading the Word daily. I wonder if they pick and choose what will make them happiest to read, rather than reading the entire thing.

You see, my God sent his Son, Jesus. Now, Jesus told us there would be trials and tribulations if we chose to follow Him. My Lord professed that it was easier for a camel to pass through the eye of a needle than for a rich man to follow Him. Paul considered it great joy to be persecuted for the sake of Christ. He rejoiced in it! And yet, here we are in the land of the free watching tragedy happen across the ocean from our comfy couches in our homes with central air, and we think, "How terrible," "How horrific," "These people are targeting Christians!" as if it was something new. Wake up American Christians. Persecution is everywhere. And it is supposed to be a joy to share in it.

As silly as it is, due to its magnitude and lack thereof, any time I have been ridiculed for my beliefs, or lost a friend because I am a Christian, or whatever else it may have been, I am thankful. When nobody is sneaking behind my back, my light must not be shining brightly. It's a joyous occasion when someone in my home is spiritually attacked. It reminds us that we're doing things the right way.

Christians, if you want to see a difference in this world, shut up and act. Ranting your political agenda on Facebook does not shine God's light like you think it does. It merely shows how holed up in your bubble you really are. Non followers have been persecuting God's people for thousands of years, but today, your Facebook status will end it all! Okay, my sarcasm is oozing. Perhaps I should bring it down a notch, I'm just fired up.

Egypt, the Pharoah used slaves to build pyramids, amongst other things. Who were these slaves? God's people. The Roman government placed laws against early Christians and their public speech. It's why we have a fish as a symbol for Christianity today. Chinese Christians worship in caves. Bibles are not allowed in the country. Their faith is punishable by death. The same holds true in Muslim territories of Ethiopia. And these are just a few of the many examples of persecution against God's people. But when a Christian in our country is "persecuted" we scream and cry for our country's religious freedom. Whatever happened to being thankful for our ability to worship freely? I believe it won't be long before that freedom is taken away from us in this country. It won't be because of terrorists and political agendas, but because God's people in this country have lost their gratitude.

For some reason we have settled into entitlement. Mostly, because it's easy to do so. We're Christians in America. We should be allowed to do whatever, whenever, however. No. There are and will always be trials and tribulations in this world. That includes us. I'm pretty sure that means more than just your Starbucks cup not having snowflakes on it.

Christian Orphans

I once heard a story from a young man from South America. He told our church that a few years ago a youth group had visited his town. Their mission trip was to help build houses and repair roofs all while sharing the message of Jesus. And they did just that. Then they left. His town never saw those people again. His hometown learned that Jesus wants you to say a prayer, help build houses, tell others to say the prayer and never see them again. What kind of message did they send? How is that considered making disciples?

It was at that point in my childhood I decided that I would not be going on a mission trip with any youth group. I knew our church had gone and done similar trips. I couldn't even think about doing that to another group of people. As this man spoke, you could hear the pain in his voice. He had the opportunity to learn the truth about Jesus when he left his town. He learned that the group that visited did not mean to cause harm. The youth group thought they were doing something for the Lord. They had no idea how much they had hurt the village. However, the people there that had accepted Jesus didn't know what to do afterwards. They weren't trained. They weren't discipled. They didn't even have a way to contact the church that had come to tell them about Jesus. A group of teenagers did a great thing. They shared the love of Jesus with a group of people who needed it. They even showed His love by helping their community and living situations. Those teenagers truly helped that village. And then they did the worst thing they could do. The group left the village never to return again. They never contacted them after they got back to the states. This youth group told a group of people that Jesus wants you to ask for His forgiveness. Jesus wants you to choose Him over everything. If you pray to Jesus that you will ask Him to forgive you, you get to go to heaven. And that's it. They left out the rest. How is this village going to grow? What happens when something happens in their village? Does Jesus still love them? Is He mad at them? Where are the answers?

The worst thing any Christian with the intension of winning people for Christ can do is give just a quick "come to Jesus" speech and let those they're speaking to figure out the rest.

Mission fields across the seas are not the only places that this can be seen. This happens regularly in our churches. My husband was dealt with in a similar manner. I had entrusted him to some friends from college. He began to go to church and even Sunday school. He met one on one with people. Soon my husband made a choice. He chose to follow Jesus. This choice came at the same time that one of those influential men took a job three hours away. Another had a pregnant wife and was consumed with family.

There's a picture painted every time I think of this situation. A baby is left on the street corner. The baby must grow up in the world he is placed in. There are people walking by that can help and more that can hurt. The baby is to grow into a boy and then a young man. He must mature into an adult quickly. How? Children in homes are fed by their parents or guardians. How will this little one get food on his own? Children in homes are taught to crawl, walk, run, and speak.

If I left a child on a street corner and said, you can come back and live with us when you figure it all out, I would be arrested. We don't treat children this way. But when we teach others about God and they become spiritual babies, are we taking them in and teaching them? Too often we are leaving them cold and afraid on the corner of the street with a "good job" sticker and a high five.

The church becomes an orphanage for those spiritual babies. One person feeds them once a week. Maybe they begin to go to small groups and bible studies. But if our spiritual parents leave us, who will become our adopted parents? Or do we have any at all?

My husband was left with many questions. Questions that I answered. I didn't mind the questions. I didn't mind providing answers. However, in a spiritual household I'm not supposed to be the spiritual leader. My husband is. I don't know how to teach him to be the spiritual leader unless I tell him how to do it, or show him how. That I was uncomfortable with. I know what you're thinking, "He could just meet with someone. Why didn't he just ask someone to meet with him?" For the same reason people who want to work out and get fit don't go to the gym sometimes. Fear. Fear of judgment. Fear of insults. Insecurities. And so much more.

Church, let us not be orphanages. And worse, let us not be orphan makers. Our job is to make disciples of all nations, not spiritual babies on street corners.

Little Ones

As adults we should take responsibility for teaching those around us, particularly those "under" us. That could be our own children, students we teach, or anyone that comes under our wings. It's a great thing to do, if we know what we're doing. But so often those "little ones" teach us something far more.

I enjoy my time with my children so much. That might be an understatement. But the more time I spend with them and invest into them, the more I see how they have taught me, changed me, and forced me to grow. When Christ said that we should have faith like a child, it is often hard to understand until you are around those children. Being a parent has shown me exactly what faith can and should look like. My husband has been the one to lead the family in throwing our children into the air. Sometimes they leave his grasp and are nine feet in the air. All they do is giggle and scream with joy. They don't fear that their father will drop them. They don't fear that he will miss them and let them fall. How often do we end up in a situation where we are tossed in the air? The first thing we do is scream, fear, and flail. We don't know why we're up in the air so we panic. But if we stop our fear and replace it with faith, we settle into that toss and know that God is going to catch us. I have watched the moment when my son was too old to be thrown. As my husband threw him, he became afraid and moved his arms in panic. My husband struggled to catch him because he had moved his position so much, but he did in fact catch him. I don't think I need to unpack that one. You get the gist.

Another great way that my children have taught me has been in prayer. My sweet daughter prays all the time. When she does, she prays in expectation. One morning she said her good morning prayer as such: "Dear Jesus, thank you for my family. Thank you for going to the playground. Pray Jesus, Amen." Okay, be kind to her she was a young two year old. But that simple prayer taught me something. She prays in expectation. Oh how I want to do that. I have tried. You see, I never said we were going to the playground. She knew she wanted to go and prayed without a doubt that I would take her. Why don't we pray like that? Why don't we thank God for the things He will bring into our lives?

My son and I were recently talking. He told me he wasn't any good at praying. That statement made me giggle after the fact. Don't let him pray for dinner if you're hungry, he's like an old preacher before the benediction. "And God… And Lord… And Jesus…" So to hear him say those words made me wonder why he thinks that. He already knows that prayer is just communication with God. So I asked him why he thinks that, and he told me, "I just don't know what to say sometimes." I explained how that happens to many people. I asked him if he thinks God hears his prayers, and this I am thankful will be written on paper. He responded with, "Yes, I hear Jesus saying my prayer to God, and sometimes I hear God answer. But, it's like a voice in my head." Woah. How many times are our thoughts and inner monologues getting in the way of the voice of God? He is stopping and listening to what Jesus says to God, and waiting for a reply from our heavenly father.

I'm not sure about you, but I'd call myself a selfish pray-er. I would rather talk at God over and over without stopping to listen. Even when I'm thanking Him for all He's given me and all He's done, I don't stop to listen. When I'm praying for other people, not a breath of space is left for His response. Wow that is selfish. Then here is this six year old telling me that he isn't good at praying when he is the one actually allowing for communication, rather than a one way street of blah, blah, blah. Sometimes I just have to stop and be still. I need to not say a word, but rest in the quiet peace of God. I have to stop to listen to Him. We all do.

Also, I love the way that young children apologize. My kids will do something stupid and immediately say, "I'm sorry, Mom." (Like the balloon that keeps flying at me while I type this.) Kids know when things aren't right. They haven't been jaded and taught to lie or cover things up. They don't have crazy elaborate excuses for something simple they have done wrong. They just know it is wrong and they are quick to apologize. I have watched kids get hit, are told sorry, and hug and make up all within about a minute and thirty seconds. Just as quickly as they apologize, they will also forgive.

There's no need to hold a grudge. If someone apologizes to them, they forgive and move on. Yet we still hold on to anger towards that person from high school that we will probably never even see again.

God uses these kids so often. I feel like such a terrible mother sometimes when I see how wonderfully these kids walk in faith. My two year old knows that Jesus is with us, and doesn't skip a beat. My son asks for prayer over him the night before a spelling bee. They aren't ashamed. They aren't afraid. If my faith, love, forgiveness, prayer, and hope were like theirs, I might just be unstoppable. How much more can we learn from the little ones?

What is Love?

I spent a lot of my life looking for love. I know what you're thinking, the end of this piece is going to end in "the answer is Jesus". Wrong. Not that Jesus isn't the answer to finding love, but I want to look at something else. There is something within us that even while walking as close as can be with the Lord, we are longing. Please don't misunderstand me in this. God, Jesus, the trinity of divinity satisfy all needs. However, what I am saying is that God designed us for relationships.

The major relationship is, of course, the one we have with God. That relationship alone dictates our lives. Outside of that, we are still wanting and designed for the company of others. This is shown to us in scripture repeatedly. We see this in the beginning. Adam is without another human. And with this, God creates Eve. This shows how our relationships of love and marriage are something from God. He planned for a man and a woman to be together in all aspects. This love of a man and woman is discussed continually throughout the Bible. Yet again, this is not the love relationship I want to discuss at the moment.

I want to talk about love between each person. That *phileo* love. Brotherly love. Love between friends, family, and importantly, Christians. How often do you sit with a Christian friend talking about life and problems, things of our daily lifestyle when all of the sudden the conversation changed. Now we are talking about Jenny and what she did and who she did it with. Without hesitation we take another person's life and make it the topic of our gossip. It is not our job to judge, condemn, or even discuss. This is exactly what we need to look at.

Do you have any idea what our role actually is? If you do, do you have any conviction to do anything about it? I ask you to honestly examine yourself through this. This isn't just my opinion or observation. It's straight from scripture. I feel so strongly convicted that I must share it, I cannot help but write it. I know you can read the bible yourself, but sometimes it helps to hear it in a different form.

This truth is written by the saint Paul. Galatians shows us what a true friend is. When we look at Galatians 6 we see that we are to bear one another's burdens. When another sins, we are not to rub it in their face. We aren't to criticize them. By no means do we discuss this person's actions with a friend while sipping our latte at the local coffee shop. In fact, what we are to do is to restore them gently (6:1). Hold up. I have to restore him? So what does that mean? Quite simply, help him out of that sin. Don't let him roll around in it, pick him up, dust him off, and keep him away from it. Paul does give a good warning which we must heed. "But watch yourself or you also may be tempted." Aha! There it is! Could it be that the reason we don't help people out of their sin is because we may be dragged down into it just as quickly? It is easier to judge from the sidelines than to battle on the field. Our world is not ESPN. We do not need more commentators. We need more players! Let's take a look back at Galatians 6, in the next verse. We've already seen that we are to carry each other's burdens, but why? When you do this, you fulfill the law of Christ. That's it. You are doing what you are supposed to do. You are fulfilling Christ's law. A New Testament realm law.

Can you imagine the feeling you get by fulfilling this law? You know that you're doing something pleasing towards God. On top of that you rescued a brother or sister from the sin that has been plaguing their life. I can only imagine that it would be like rescue diving. Dropping into the water, swimming towards the drowning victim. As you snatch them and begin to swim back to the helicopter you notice sharks close by. You grab onto the cable, hooking yourself and the victim to the cable. They hoist you up. As your foot comes out of the water, a great white charges toward you out of the water almost taking you and your victim. But now you are safe. The helpless victim owes their life to your bravery and courage. To you, it's just doing your job.

Picture that in the spiritual realm. Your friend is drowning in the sin of _____. (Fill it in: lust, drunkenness, gossip, adultery, etc.) And instead of sitting on the beach calling 911, you go in and save them. Prayer is good. Prayer works. But sometimes you also need to get in there. Battle. Fight. Carry their load so that can stand again.

There are so many times that we are in the position of the one caught in sin. Sometimes that temptation, pressure, rebellion, is too much for us. So instead of fighting through, we give in. Over and over. Each time we give in, we feel worse and worse, and we need to continue in sin to distract us from guilt or conviction. There are so many times that I am down and out. My sin takes me to a place I do not want to be in. But I stay in that place because it's easy, and usually fun. I know I need to get out, but I find my self-loathing creates a need to be accepted. My sin gives me that acceptance and welcomes me in. It is only when I come to another person that I get out of my sin. Someone that not only prays for me, but asks about it. Have I been in that sin? How am I doing with it? Has there been temptation for it, opportunities for it? Often times it is the people that say, "Call me when you feel you want to go back that way" that help the most. Because even a phone call will keep me from taking that opportunity that has come around. This, my friends, is love. Taking on someone's burdens, strife, and heartache in the midst of your own worries and life. Christ says this, "No greater love there is, than when a man lays his life down for another." (John 15:13) We so often think that it means taking a bullet for someone. Perhaps it means a father giving a kidney to his daughter, or some other ailment/treatment scenario.

What about this: Do we ever think that laying our lives down could mean we stop what we are doing in the middle of the day for someone else? Maybe it means missing your favorite TV show to talk to someone on the phone who needs an ear.

Maybe it means you give up your daily workout to drive someone who doesn't have a car. Maybe it means giving up your lunch hour to take your daughter to the mall for some bonding time. When we give up what we want for another person, and help them with their needs, then it is love.

So I guess my point in all of this is that I know why I'm looking for love. I look because I am looking for someone unselfish. Jesus has been the only one. My parents love me. My family as well. Do my friends? If you ever wonder why I don't like big groups of friends, this is it. You don't get that unselfish love. At least I haven't seen it. More importantly, am I doing it?

I Can Save Him!

I'm not sure why, but it seems like most people go through a stage where they feel like they can fix the broken people of the world. Too often it's in regards to the person they are dating. The truth behind it is that we really just want to be with them and know that their issues aren't what we want to drag into a relationship, but we figure if we change them we can have our cake and eat it too. Don't lie, you know there is one person you have either tried to change or wanted to try to change.

As a Christian, this is a challenging situation to be in. I know it firsthand. There's that one person that catches your attention. You step back and weigh the pros and cons. In the end, there is just one thing that keeps you two apart. So what do we do? We say, "I'll help them see the right way. People change. I can be the one to change them."

Now when it comes to the big one, you know, the one where the other person either is or is not a Christian, it's a whole different set of statements. The big one is, "Maybe I'm supposed to be with them so I can witness to them. They can find Jesus through me." Hmm. Well, we don't want to be downers, but the truth is that it is rare that the person we date comes to Jesus because of us. I know this first hand. I have had boyfriends that did not find Jesus and two that did. The odds were not in my favor.

It's a struggle when you're dating someone whose only flaw is not knowing Jesus. It's different though, isn't it? We want them to be with us. "They're perfect, except for…" I know it. Don't you think I know it? And then we hear the words, "go and make disciples" ringing in our heads. See! We should be with them so that we can bring them to Christ. I would like to agree with that. But if there is one thing I know, it's that Scripture holds true.

Take a walk with me to two very important verses in the Bible. 1 Corinthians 15:33 tells us very plainly, "Do not be deceived: bad company corrupts good morals." Gulp. So I guess being around people without my good morals will just bring me down versus me bringing them up. I know your argument, don't even try it. How are we supposed to witness to people if we can't be around bad company? Look, we are to go into the world. We are to work with them, love them, and show Christ to them. But we don't need to date them and let them into the most intimate parts of our lives. That verse is telling us that the bad rubs off onto people faster than the good can clean it off. We tell ourselves it won't happen to us. We tell ourselves that we are too grounded. Look, get a grip. You aren't the first person that came out a little more rough after you were around the wrong people. Do you think you are the only person that started good and went to hang out with the bad kids? Please! Don't flatter yourself. This is a common problem. That's why Paul wrote it. He saw it over 2,000 years ago.

The second verse we need to keep is close is 2 Corinthians 6:14. "Do not be bound together with unbelievers; for what partnership has righteousness and lawlessness, or what fellowship has light with darkness?" This one gets me a little deeper. The word bound really hits home when it comes to dating. See, we can be around non-Christians, we have to be. But when we have the choice, we should choose to not bind ourselves to those who aren't with God. I struggle with the righteousness to lawlessness. Probably because I don't always see myself as righteous. I'm close to the lawlessness group, or at least in my mind. The truth is that God saved a wretch like me. Now I am righteous. And I should be a shining light. But instead I hang around the dinge and dirt too much and my light gets covered in darkness. I ask you this – will you stop and think on this verse? What does light and darkness have in common? Why are they binding themselves together? The light goes to the darkness. Darkness creeps in on light. But do they stay together? No, one always wins out.

We can't hold on to the idea that by being their significant other we can bring them to Christ. There are too many emotions and desires mixing together. I'll tell you a little story. When I was a freshman in high school I began dating a junior. Though I was a Christian, I assumed a few things like I wouldn't find my husband in high school and that dating whoever didn't really matter. Years later my ex-boyfriend and I connected over lunch. He shared with me all about what was happening in his church. He then began to share the gospel message with me! I told him I had been a Christian since I gave my life to

Christ at the age of four and he was shocked. "Why did you date me, then? I wasn't a Christian. Why would you do that?" Thanks for that guilt. He knew it. I shouldn't have been bound to him.

I think sometimes we just don't see it. We just aren't mature enough to realize that we aren't going to change that person. Only the Holy Spirit can change someone. We can plant seeds. We can water. That's it. The rest is between that person and God. It can't be an ultimatum. It can't be to make you happy. It can only be through the power of the cross. I'm not saying you won't help a person reach that decision, but I am saying, don't bind your light to darkness because bad company corrupts good morals.

Drop the Zero, Get You a Hero

Oh, the dating world. What a cruel mistress she can be. I've come across some truth though. Jerry Seinfeld is a hilarious comedian. He says in one of his bits that women are changing their men. She says, "No, not my guy, he's coming along." Jerry's reply, "No. He's not." I started thinking about it, and it makes me mad at myself and all other women. We are constantly trying to change our guys and make them better. I have two points of discussion about this.

Point One: It's not your place. Stop for a second and think about the ways you're trying to change your man. Is it something minor like putting the empty soda bottle in the recycling bin? Often times, couples get into fights because of something this small. A humble loving woman companion would simply do the chore herself. Maybe he forgot. Maybe he doesn't care. Whatever it is, there is no reason to call him out on it every time. You become a nag! Eventually, he will see you doing it and realize he needs to, and he will start. Maybe you're trying to change something bigger, more important, like how he handles money or his spiritual walk and leadership in the relationship.

Who told you to be his mother? No one held a gun to your uterus and told you to be a woman did they? Then why do we pull the trigger back with every unwise decision he makes? He needs to figure it out on his own. It isn't your job to make him grow up. If he uses your thoughts and opinions along with Scripture (first and foremost) to come to his own conclusions, then fine, great, dandy. He has taken time to decide his stance. If you force your thoughts and opinions on him, what will he learn? He needs to do it on his own. Ladies, it is never our role to make our companion change. It has to be his will and desire to better himself. Maybe you're the one that needs the change. Let him mature and grow as he needs to. They do it for us. We are not always right. If he is to change, then he (with the help of the Holy Spirit) will change.

Point Two: It's not him. If you have a list of things that he needs to change, he is not what you want. He is who he is, just as you are who you are. If your man came to you and tried to change everything about you, you'd be furious. You'd go off ranting and raving about how he doesn't love you for you and he just wants you to be someone you're not. But for some strange reason we find it okay to change someone into a man they aren't either. If he has so many things that need to change, he's probably not the guy for you.

I already told you it isn't your place to change him, so why be with someone you aren't happy with? All you are doing is insulting the guy you are with. Take a second and imagine that the guy you are with changed to all the things you wanted. Is it still him?

Probably not. You are trying to make him something he isn't supposed to be. Let him be who God made him. If it's not what God has designed for you, then walk away and wait for Mr. Right. If you're already married, you just can't walk away, than evaluate your own heart. Why do you want him to be so different? The answer is usually something to do with making your life easier. Examine your motives. You are to respect and love your husband. That's even when he isn't perfect. If you can't find the good in which you married him, you are probably the one who needs changing.

Now I know a lot of this sounds harsh, but it's true. You can't spend your life trying to "better" someone. We are to love our partners. Some of you may be in harsh relationships already, where your husband is really in need of change. As much as he may need it, we must realize we aren't going to be the ones to do it. We can pray for it, and be supportive, but it is God and only God who can change a man's heart. So don't think yourself equal with God. Just be the woman you're supposed to be. The girlfriend, fiancé, wife, mother or sister in Christ that you need to be and let God be the God he promises to be.

Drop that Zero, Get You a Hero II

I am so double sided sometimes. Well, I am double sided all the time. Here I am, athletic, buff, sporty, jock. But there is nothing I enjoy more than a chick flick. That's right. I said it. I love the stupid teenie bopper girl movies where the main character gets her man.

Normally my reaction is, "This sucks. This doesn't happen in real life. No guy ever sweeps the girl off her feet and gives her a fairy tale ending." Well why not?! Because we, as women, have let them off the hook! We lowered our standards so that we aren't alone. Ladies, be a hopeless romantic. Desire a man that romances you! Long for a man that will treat you as royalty. Wait for a man that wants everything to be perfect.

Oh, did I say wait? Yeah, I did. Wait for the man that would give up anything and everything to be with you, make you happy, and make you feel special. Stop letting go of your standards to get a quick fix. Make them do what they are supposed to do. If they don't want to be your Romeo, if they don't want to wait for you at your door, if they don't want to dance under the stars with you, don't waste your time.

Men, get to work. Women, good women, take care of you. They cook, clean, rub your back, and dream of you. Not to impress you, but to love you. And you have been taking advantage of loving women. You take the relationship for all the good things you get, but when they need a loving hand, you flee because they're too emotional. If you care for a girl, prove it. Don't tell them you love them. Show them. Rub their back for once. Cook them dinner. Be romantic. Don't give women the bare minimum. Too many women have lacked self worth their entire lives. So what happens? They take anything they can get. You are to be the spiritual leaders. This means you should be there when they struggle with themselves. Don't just make them happy, tell them their worth in Christ. Show them the same love Christ shows you. Treat them like the daughters of God that they are so that they never doubt!

I recently asked myself why movie endings don't ever happen in real life. The answer came quickly. We don't let it happen. We take the first thing, not the best thing. If only we would learn to wait.

Too Strong Willed

As I write this, my daughter is now a one year old. Well, one going on twelve. She is a very active child; running, climbing, exploring. She tests the limits and boundaries constantly. And in case I've missed all of this in my everyday caretaking of her, people are ready to tell me at a moment's notice. "She's a handful!" "That girl gets into everything!" "I don't know how you get anything done with her." Thank you, observers. I was looking for someone to tell me about my daughter. The best comments come from family members. They speak to me as if my daughter's behavior is a punishment to me. "You were strong willed too, but not like this!" The voices chime.

Okay, so you're telling me that my daughter wanting to climb onto benches, open and close doors, and just try her hardest to do the things that her brother and parents do is bad? The only thing that shows me is how strong this young girl is. She teaches herself and works hard to do things that the people she looks up to do. My daughter is fearless. My daughter is strong, both physically and mentally. My daughter is resilient.

At first, my reaction to the comments was very defensive. So what if she is strong willed, she still does what is asked of her. She may battle me over and over, but I've been strong willed for longer than she has. What's the big deal if she wants to know her place, and to assert herself?

Now fast forward. I'm finishing this project as my daughter will soon be three. This child is still just as strong, but it is working out just I figured it would. She is loving and kind. She apologizes quickly, when necessary. She forgives quickly. And she will stand up for herself, and her brother. This girl will challenge someone, when necessary.

I look to the future often. I know that God will use both of my kids in big ways. Who knows when, where or how, but I know it's coming. I have a feeling my daughter's strength will have something to do with it. I feared having a daughter. I feared the pressures that she will face growing up. But by the time my daughter turned two, I knew things would be okay. She'll stand up for herself. She'll say no to the pressures that will approach her.

There are plenty of times that I turn to Joshua to read the beginning. Joshua 1:6 – "Be strong and courageous…" Joshua 1:7 – "Only be strong and very courageous…" Joshua 1:9 – "Have I not commanded you? Be strong and courageous!" Joshua 1:18 – "…; only be strong and courageous." There are so many times I wish I was stronger. I wish I had more courage. I wish I could be bold and do the things I know needed to be done. God told Joshua to walk through other people's camps. He told Joshua to go, proclaim, and take what was given. But he would not be able to unless he had strength and courage. Look, I'm thick headed. It takes a while for things to set in with me. But when the words "be strong and courageous" come up four times in 13 verses, I pay attention. You should too.

So I look at my daughter. Fear escapes her. Weakness hides. She is not out of control or unruly. She is not disobedient or stubborn. I am working with her continually to use that strength. Maybe that's you. Maybe you were a wild child. Fearless and strong willed. If that is who God made you to be, why would you be trained against it? Be strong and courageous. Walk through the enemy's camp. Claim what is yours, by the hand of God.

Being strong willed does not mean that you are on the wrong path. Being strong willed means you are the one making the path. Where is it that you have not been strong or courageous? Where have you not jumped out of the plane, all or nothing, into what you were called?

This project you're reading – this compilation of pieces I've written through the years, over a decade. Why do you think it has taken this long to write what I want and put it together? I didn't have the courage. I didn't have the strength to say what I wanted to say. That's why I'm so thankful for a strong willed daughter. She taught me to be courageous and write. I'll make my path where God has called me, despite the voices bringing me down. I hope you too will be strong and courageous to follow where God leads.

Mary

I married a Mary. Okay, easy now, don't hang me yet. My husband is a Mary, but I'm not calling him a wuss or a sissy. Look at Luke 10:38. Jesus goes to stay with Mary and Martha. Martha works herself to the bone. She's making food, doing dishes, pouring drinks, setting the table. Martha is a rock star hostess. Her sister Mary is hanging out with Jesus, just sitting at his feet.

Every time I read this passage I think two things. One: sometimes I need to put down the work to enjoy the love of the people around me. Two: What the heck, God?

Like I said, I married a Mary. My husband will always choose hanging out with guests over doing the chores of hosting. And who wouldn't? At this stage in my life I am taking care of two kids full time, while working from home. It's hard. My to-do lists stretch longer than I ever imagined possible. How do you become a great personal trainer? You train and learn, continually. How do you become a better writer, a successful writer? You write, always. So on top of diaper changes/potty training, laundry folding, cleaning, writing, training, tutoring, and everything else, I am supposed to be spending time with God, family, and friends.

In case you haven't figured it out, I'm a Martha. To many, that to-do list looks daunting, impossible even. To me it's exciting. I wear my list like a badge of honor. "Look at me! Look at me! I did all these things! See what I did? Appreciate me! Love me! Be in awe of me!" Wait, what? Isn't that the heart of Marthas near and far? Past, present and future?

Let's look at what *the* Martha says. "Lord, do you not care that my sister has left me to do all the serving alone? Tell her to help me." In other words, "Hey teacher, you see me right? I'm doing it all." I think Martha was expecting a different answer. Something like, "Oh Martha! Great job! You've been working so hard. Come sit. Mary can finish the work." Marthas, like myself, want to be a part of the group too, but we're better at doing the work. But when we do that work, we want affirmation in front of the group. "Oooh," "Ahh," gasps and jealous whispers are the things we Marthas enjoy.

Over the years I have learned to be less of a Martha and more of a Mary. On my crazy to-do list there isn't always a set deadline. I get things done, when kids are napping or having downtime. I take clients when my husband is home as often as possible so that I can spend time with what matters, or rather who matters. My back is sore, my legs are tired, but sitting on the floor with kids far out-weighs working while they sit in front of the TV.

Then again, here comes that second thought I have. What the heck, God? Martha cooks dinner and then is told that Mary chose what was right. Well if Martha didn't get dinner done and the table set, who would? Okay, let's take a time out. If Jesus was sitting in my house, I would assume that He could whip something up in the miracle cookbook. But He didn't. He didn't offer. Maybe He never offered to perform the miracle because He wasn't given the chance. Martha filled in with some cooked salmon and Jesus didn't do a miracle. Woah. That's weighty. Sometimes, as Marthas, we don't get to experience miracles because we do our version of the work before Jesus gets His chance to do His work. Ouch. That just hit me a little too hard.

My Marthas are speaking to me now, "Yes, but Jesus isn't sitting on my couch. I need to cook dinner for my family or we are all going to starve." Okay, true, the "in the flesh" Jesus isn't on your couch, but He is in your home. And sometimes the best dinners I have made were when I whipped something up quick because I had forgotten my wifely and motherly duties to be a wife and a mother on the floor playing or out at the playground.

Marthas, it may be hard, but every so often choose to be a Mary. Look at those around you and ask yourself how you can sit at the feet of Jesus with them. Dinner will take care of itself.

Death Comes

Every parent wants to die before their children do. Honestly, who wants to see their child pass before their time. I'm like that. Always have been, but not just my children. I have always said I want to die before my husband, my brother, parents. It's just all too much for me. But the most absurd thing that I said was that I want to die before my grandparents. That seems very illogical I know this, but it's the connection I've had with them. It's the way they have always been there and have kept things calm. They have meant so much that I just couldn't imagine my life without them.

But here comes the bad news. Reality is winning. My grandfather (Frumps as we have loving called him for about 30 years and counting) found out he had a spot on his pancreas, according to an MRI. Meaning of this spot- cancer. It really hit me hard. This, of course, made me feel like a bad person. You see, my other grandfather died when I was 12. I never cried. I tried. I cared. I loved him. But there is something that has always kept me from being emotional. I say the difference in the two lies in two parts. The first is that I was able to form a more substantial bond with Frumps by living near him in my teenage years. He came by the house. I went to theirs. He came to all my sporting events – something my mother thinks would have helped the bond with the other grandfather. He even saw a college game in Virginia. We shared something. And I always knew he was proud of me. The second is that they both had cancer. However, they were completely different. My late grandfather didn't die from the lung cancer, it was complications of a stroke later in time. Frumps had pancreatic cancer. And he was one of the healthiest 87 year old men you could find. He rode his stationary bike, did yard work, and gave all who entered his home an ice cream sandwich – even for breakfast.

So I guess what I'm getting to is that I didn't understand why this would happen to him. And I know the right answers – God's will, God's sovereignty, God's grace etc. But as we all know, it won't be for a long time until we know and understand why things happen.

There is another major difference between my grandfathers. When my late grandfather was on his deathbed I couldn't fathom him dying because we never knew if he became a believer before the end. Even at a young age the only thing I could pray was that he found God before he passed. On the other hand, I didn't want Frumps to die for selfish reasons. I want him here. I want him to mumble and not hear the prayer at Thanksgiving dinner. I wanted him to be healthy enough to see me get married. I'm selfish. I want my grandfather back. I'm not sure how everyone else has gone through this.

I've had to edit the writings above, as it was written before April 2010. I write this now in 2017.

Frumps passed away October 1, 2010. I was there. His younger sister was in the room, as was my father. It was a heart wrenching time for us, especially as I was 4 months pregnant. My grandmother passed just weeks later. Broken heart syndrome. That's the effect Frumps had on people. And let me tell you, it was his heart for the Lord. His death brought three more people to Christ. He did work for the kingdom even when he was no longer with us. What a legacy!

I now have two children, a loving husband, all parents, and one grandparent. A brother and brother in law with sister in laws and a niece and two nephews are also present in my life. And even now, I do things with a mindset that I want to make my grandparents proud. It's not because they will see and give me a good report in heaven. It's because I know the impact they had on the people around them, and I want to have that type of impact. I want my life to count for something even when I'm gone. I look at my children and KNOW that they will do great things. I no longer want to die young so I don't have to experience loss. I want to live as long as possible and see the wonders that are done.

Take on Hell with a Squirt Gun

Death. It's everywhere. It is one of the major fears of Americans. Why? Because we fear the unknown. Well what about Christians? Do we fear death? Many Christians would not fear death. They are excited. Some say, "I can't wait for the Father to take me from this world." Still some Christians don't fear death, but do not want to die. They want to complete more work before they go. They want to touch one more life. They want to complete one more work before they go. They want to touch one more life. They want to be a part of one more disciple on earth. To those Christians: I commend you.

You are far better than me. I fear death. I do not fear being killed. I do not fear being on my death bed. I fear my life thus far has been a waste. I had once attended a memorial service for a football player at my university. Everyone who knew him was significantly affected by him. They miss his smile. They miss his leadership, his friendship, him. They miss all of him. Everything that made him who he was. I started to think about what it would be like to lose someone close to me, which I now truly have. But then I took all of this one step further. If I were to die in my sleep, or the next time I was in the car, how would I be remembered?

That is my fear of death. When I am gone, what kind of impact will I have on the people around me? I evaluate my recent conversations. I go back to the last time I talked to certain people. What was said? Did I offend them? Was I sarcastic or rude? Did I unload my problems on them? How is that one person going to remember me? Sometimes I have this thought that when I die, the people at my service will all get up, singing "Ding dong the witch is dead! Which old witch? The wicked witch!" It scares me. It puts a gut-wrenching fear in the pit of my stomach.

I could tell you how I want to be remembered. I could give my own eulogy, but what good is that? People may be saying, "Why do you care what other people think of you?" Well, nothing, if it's my choice of sporting apparel or jeans, or my makeup style. However, I do care a good deal about what people think about my life. I am a follower of Christ. The bar has been set for me. Am I living up to it, or missing the mark? As cliché as it may be by now, I may be the only Jesus someone sees. Do I live a life that draws them to the Father or one that makes non-believers happy they aren't Christians? Will I be remembered as loving, sweet spirited, encouraging, faithful, graceful with a beautiful soul? I fear death. I fear that I will leave the wrong mark on someone and I can never make it right, apologize, and repair the situation.

But it is at this point I have a revelation. God takes the care of all things. He will take me when I am needed to leave. People will hear from me what they are going to hear. God will use it as He wishes, for He is God. So then you might be thinking, "What was the point of all this if it comes down to God taking care of all things?" Simple. God desires Christians to realize that we are being watched. Our classmates, teammates, professors, coworkers, bosses, employees, friends and families are watching us. What we do and say can be held into consideration when someone comes to the point of a decision. My legacy, should not be a fear of entrapment, but encouragement. I have a reason to live out. I can check my heart, motivation, words and actions everyday and moment to make sure I am going to be remembered well. And if not, it shows where I need more help from the Lord.

Discipline

When you hear the word "discipline" what do you do? Do you cringe and fold up waiting for the next round of spankings? Do you automatically picture the little kid in the grocery store who is throwing a tantrum? I've always had a firm stance in discipline. Proverbs says, "Spare the rod, spoil the child." My parents believed in that. They were strong disciplinarians. I took this version of parenting as well. I'm not making any distinctions on what discipline is. There will be no discussion on spanking vs. time out. If you feel the need to discuss you can reach me at my website (jjsweeney.weebly.com). Discipline, be it time out, spankings, or a stern voice, is necessary for growth.

For a long enough time I knew that discipline was necessary. Kids need to know right from wrong. They need to learn at a young age. They need to figure out how to act, speak, work, etc. After meeting a parent that refused to discipline their child and claimed Christ as Lord, it made me think. The Bible states, "God disciplines those He loves." If we are to be godly, we need to instill discipline into our children's lives.

We need that discipline as well. There have been many times that I have seen doors close, opportunities lost, and parts of life that seemed ripped out from underneath me. It takes some time, but I soon realize it is all a part of God's will, and sometimes that means his divine discipline. Some of those things that were wrongfully taken from me, weren't wrongful at all. Some things were taken because I didn't use them properly. Others were taken because God knew what choices I would have made if things didn't change. If we aren't watching, discipline from God often looks like an attack from Satan.

I remember as a teen the phrases we heard jokingly were, "This hurts me more than it hurts you," and "I'm doing this for your own good." No, we weren't getting disciplined, it was always a joke, but there is a lot of truth in that. When you are disciplining a child, it is for their own good. And often, it really does hurt you more than it hurts them. That's why there are so many unruly children. Being the reason your child cries, even though we know they need the lesson learned, hurts. It stinks. It breaks your heart little by little.

Now place yourself in God's shoes. He wants what is best for us. He wants us to become the best version of ourselves that we can possibly be. Sometimes that means He has to discipline us. If it hurts me to have to discipline two children, how does God feel disciplining all of us? But He knows he needs to. He must do what is right for us to learn a new lesson. For some of us that takes longer. Sometimes we need the bricks to fall on our heads.

If we stay in the spirit and walk with God, we can better assess the situation. We can see where God is guiding us, moving us, and allowing doors to close. It will still be painful, but we understand it. My two year old doesn't always grasp the concept of discipline, but my six year old does. He knows that sometimes he doesn't get what he wants because he has done something wrong. Yes, that happens to us. We know we mess up. Thankfully we have a God that will discipline us and guide us back to the path we must take.

It's funny. When I don't feel God with me as my disciplinarian, I get scared. A decade ago my attitude was different. If I didn't feel a hand of guidance, or the stern voice, or the flat out smack upside the head, I thought I was sitting pretty. Now that I've got some more life experience I can see that when I don't feel God's discipline every once in a while I worry that I've walked too far away from His will for the discipline to come. That's usually when I dive more into His word and focus on my deliberate time with Him. And yes, I find the areas that I need to work on almost immediately.

One thing I've learned, as a parent and as a Christian, is that discipline isn't as harsh when the offense isn't so large. The adage "the punishment fits the crime" holds true when true discipline is dispatched. And the wise ones learn quickly that discipline is a great form of love.

Bueller, Bueller? – Hello, McFly?

Complacent Christians. What do they look like? We hear about them all the time. We often find ourselves to be them, but what is it? How can we find it before it hits us?

As I prayed for a friend's living situation, I had a revelation. My friend is recently married (7 months). When they got married, the couple settled down in a small town near family. Though they moved just a few hours from their home, they are right down the road from the family members. They are familiar with people in the area. They even went on a mission trip with some people from the family's church.

When they moved, they were very excited. Then the school year started up. Their cousins are all busy which means their parents are too. So the whole family is quite busy and my friend rarely sees them anymore. Many of their friends from mission trip went back to college or are working hard as they are. It is rare that the couple have company over, because of everyone's schedules. The couple does have one good friend who visits often. However, this friend is moving away. Soon they will be left alone again.

I say this because my friends are ready and willing to move back home. It is too hard for them to make it out there. Things are uncomfortable. They would much rather go home where they have his parents, mutual friends, family and a church. They want to be surrounded by what they know.

When I think of this scenario, I wonder – How much is this like many Christians today? We like the new atmosphere in the beginning. But once life picks up again, things get hard. The same people aren't around. People move, get busy. We are left to work out our faith in a new way. This brings fear.

We want to go back to the way things were. We want to be comfortable. We want to be where we know we can survive. But that isn't always the best answer. How do we grow if we are not challenged? It is through the tough times that survival is greatest.

There's a beautiful song by Hawk Nelson called, "He's making diamonds out of us." Okay, don't tell them this because I love Hawk Nelson, but I don't really care for the music of the song. It's too blah, regular ordinary. But the lyrics of the song are perfect. "He is refining in his timing, He's making diamonds out of us." When I think about that process of how diamonds are made I'm reminded to press on. Diamonds are made of pressure and heat. And here we are, as Christians, getting an ounce of uncomfortable situations and we're out. We run away. Our faith would be so much more if we would fight through the pressure.

Now these friends I spoke of did in fact move back. They did become comfortable. I believe they got a little too comfortable and allowed for things of the world to creep in. Eventually, they got a divorce and parted ways for good. I sometimes wonder what would have happened if they had stuck it out in that place further from their comfort. What would life be like if they stayed and plugged in, despite the difficulty of it all? Would they have stayed together? Would they have changed their lifestyles? I'll never know.

I can speak only of myself at this point. When my husband and I have experienced difficult points of life we have turned into ourselves, deep within to our heart of hearts. We have prayed and fought. Things don't always play out perfectly, but we know that we are better people, better spouses, better parents, better workers, all because we have gone through the fire. There will be more problems. There will be more pressures and the heat will hit, but we will not run anywhere, unless it is running toward God, through the valley.

Freedom

My pastor ended a sermon by asking, "Do you want to be free from your chains?" The response was silence. And we aren't your average nod and smile church. People give their "Amens, mmhmms, and yes'!" We finish his sentences and repeat Scripture with him. In our church, voices are heard and encouraged. So why the silence?

I have two theories. The first is my hope, though I fear it has less to do with it. The silence may have come from the conviction of it all. He shared a video that was quite compelling. An elephant in the parking lot of a circus doesn't run away. Why? The elephant is chained to a stick in the ground. The elephant could easily kick his leg and be free, but he doesn't. Instead he stands patiently waiting for the circus workers to lead it around for its performance.

That's what so many, countless, Christians are doing with their lives. We have the power of God within us and we choose to stand in the parking lot of our lives chained to a stick. Such a vivid metaphor. I think after we watched that video we were all doing a gut check. Throughout the congregation, silence fell as we asked ourselves if we were chained to a stick. It's hard to give a heartfelt "Yes" when you're searching your soul for the chains that bind you.

But I have a lot of doubt in this first theory, so I give you my second. We're cowards. Sorry, but I can't lie. We were going through our church's "word of the year," courage. And that is exactly what we need. Ask over 100 people if they are ready for the freedom from the chains that bind them and the answer with silence and I say COWARDS!

I'm harsh, I know, but hear me out. Why would we give up those chains? Freedom! Woohoo! I'm free! Now what? The elephant doesn't break the chain because he's scared. The last time he sought freedom he was probably beaten with a stick and tasered. I bet if we left that chain on him, but didn't secure it to anything he would still stand there. The fear of freedom will keep that animal right where he is.

The fear of freedom is a fear we live in as Christians and we need to let it go. When we live in freedom we fear falling back to the chains. We fear those around us. We fear our brothers and sisters in Christ will think we weren't sincere. We worry that they non-Christians will come at us with the sticks and tasers ready to beat us back into submission. And at the end of the day, sometimes we're afraid of where to go and what to do. When we are finally out of the chains we will be expected to run. People will see our freedom and want to know where we will go and what we will do, now that we aren't bound.

Honestly, we don't know, do we? I, for one, have battled with lies of my self-worth for more years than I can count. Even now that I am happily married with two children, I struggle to believe that I am a person who can be loved by anyone else. It makes no sense, but sometimes it's easier. It is easier for me to go crawl back into my hole and hide than for me to stand up and say, "My husband, my son, and my daughter love me for me." What happens when I live in that freedom, when I know deep within me that I am loved not just by my God, but by my family? I'm a woman like no other. My job as wife and mother becomes my blessing. I am more supportive, caring, loving. I clean messes and wipe noses and stay up late and get up early with a smile on my face. Why is that so scary? I don't know, but it is. Maybe I'm afraid it won't last and I'll be a bad mother or wife. Maybe I'm afraid that my best still isn't good enough. That's the type of soul searching that keeps me from giving a "Yes" when I'm asked if I want freedom.

This isn't how it should be. We don't exchange bondage for fear. Fear is just a new chain. We can be free. We can walk away. We can run from those chains and never look back. Sometimes I think we take the chain from the wall it is bound to, but never take the chain off ourselves. We walk around with the chains dragging along behind us ready to attach them to the next prison cell we come across. Most of us aren't taking off the shackles for our freedom, but that's what God wants for us. He wants us to saw them off and leave them behind.

I often see the dragging of our chains. It can be disguised as weakness. It makes the wearer look like a victim. You've seen them too, haven't you? They reveal their past, be it painful, embarrassing, or scary. They tell you how they have overcome the troubles of this world. Then they tell you again. And again. And again. And it seems like the past they have gotten over is still there. They wake up with it every morning even though it's been gone for weeks, months, or years. They drag that chain and it snags on rocks and roots along the way tripping them up.

When we are free in Christ, we are free indeed. So choose freedom over fear. Choose freedom over comfort. Don't just take the chains off the wall. Take off the chains. Run away, hard and fast, into the arms of Christ. Keep yourself from tripping on those chains again.

The Struggle is Real

Romans 5 is one of my favorite chapters in the Bible. Through the years, I have found myself drawn to verses 2-5. I've used it continually within my struggles. It gives me strength. My suffering brings perseverance or endurance. That builds character, some versions say, "proven character." And character produces hope which "does not put us to shame." Wow. What power in those words!

One morning I had a spiritual thought as I wrote that verse in my journal. Why don't we do that for our children? There are so many times that we do for our children and never allow them to do things for themselves.

Today we complain, continually, that teens and young adults have no character. They have no morals, values, or the biggest, work ethic. Of course they don't! How are our children supposed to have good work ethic if they are never challenged to do any work? I see helicopter parents everywhere. They need to be in their child's business for every detail of life. I've watched parents complain and yell at teachers because the work is "too hard" or "too much" for their child. Schools give less homework today than they have since the pioneer days. Get over it and get over your kid.

How many times do we see the parents that hold their kids back, not because their child needs it, but for their own satisfaction? I get it. I feel like the other day I was rocking my son to sleep and now he's off in school. They grow up quick. But so did we. Our parents had to go through it. And their parents. So on and so forth. My parents didn't keep me from milestones because they weren't ready for their baby to move on. But I see it all the time. Mama Bears aren't ready for the cub to catch its own fish, so Mama Bear catches it, skins it, debones it, chews it up and feeds it to the cub, who is far too old for that.

Why do parents do it? Why do friends do it? Why do siblings do it? Well, one theory is that parents are selfish and don't want their kids to grow up. But I don't believe that's always what it is. It isn't just parents. Parents love their kids more than anything else in the world. The last thing they truly want is for their child to be behind. They're trying to protect them. We do that as friends as well. We know what the world has to offer. We know pain and heartache. If we can keep our children as babies they won't have all that. They only need to know our love. If we keep that girl away from that guy she won't feel rejection. They'll know we have their back.

That's not what Scripture is teaching us. No, Paul wrote to the church in Rome that we should rejoice in our suffering. As parents and loved ones, we're okay taking the suffering. We're okay learning perseverance and building character. We've done it before. But when parents keep children from hard times, what do they learn? We take away the issues that kids need in order to deal with life as adults.

Parents spend so much time protecting their kids from things they don't like that children are not suffering from anything.

If there is no suffering, there is no endurance. If there is no endurance, there is no proven character. That should be enough right there. My children will be known for their character, I can promise you that. But Paul adds one more thing to the list. Character produces hope. It's a hope that does not put us to shame. I want that. I want that for me. I want that for my family, those here now and yet to come.

I came to the decision before I focused on this passage, but reading it again in this new light puts words to my actions. It used to be about that "old school" way of parenting. Don't give in to the kids. Don't let them run the show. It isn't going to kill them. But now I see it as God intended. I allow my children to experience difficulties, and sometimes pain. Maybe that's why people tell me my kids are "advanced." I don't see it. I think they are exactly where they should be. They have pushed their way through only to learn to hope for more in life. Not everyone goes through hard times in the same sense of the word. We should be there for people when they just can't pull themselves from the muck. But we can't do everything for them. They need to learn to endure and persevere.

No door is closed unless God closes it. People can deal with closed doors and unexpected twists and turns in life from enduring a few hard times growing up. I'm not a parenting expert by any means. I can't force my opinion on people, but I will say this: When I look at my kids, I see them now and I imagine what they will be when they are older. I think about middle school, high school, adulthood. How will they handle sticky situations? When something doesn't go their way are they going to stomp their feet and whine or are they going to endure?

It's my job, and every parent's job, every friend's job, to teach Romans 5 to their children and loved ones. Find it joy to suffer. Persevere through it all for character that produces hope. A hope that keeps us together.

I'm not saying we don't protect our children and friends, but we can't fight all their battles. Let them in the ring. You might be surprised by what they can do.

Farewell

Thank you for taking this walk with me. I know that some of it may sound redundant. Some of you may think that I have issues. Well, I do. We all do. That's the beauty of Jesus. He is the author and FINISHER of our faith. This is just a journey we all must take. Though we all have our issues, our sins, our struggles, we can all rely on the same Jesus that will be the perfecter of it all. We just need to keep walking with him.

I hope that something I wrote sat within your soul the way it has with me. I pray that I have been an example of Hebrews 10:24. I pray that you will be stirred to love and good works. I hope that you will run the race set before you and that you rest only in the presence of the King. I know that there will be more to come, whether in book or blog or whatever God has in place. I have been called to speak, I am so grateful for this opportunity to speak to you.

58730229R00078

Made in the USA
Columbia, SC
24 May 2019